"In bravely revealing his thoughts, insights, and m in the field of autism and sexuality, Nick Dubin has turned a devast: involvement with the criminal justice system into an educational and learning experience. A must-read for anyone supporting those on the autism spectrum in the vital area of sexuality."

> —*Stephen M. Shore, Ed.D., Clinical Assistant Professor of Special Education at Adelphi University, internationally known consultant, educator, and author on issues related to the autism spectrum*

"I was deeply moved by Nick Dubin's candid account of his frightening experience in the criminal justice system. This compelling and informative book shows how prosecutors can overreach in their pursuit of a criminal conviction with devastating consequences to individuals on the autism spectrum and their families. Hopefully, this seminal work will shed some light on a long neglected subject and jumpstart a discussion in the legal system that includes compassion and understanding."

> —*Bradley Schram, former Prosecutor and Founding Shareholder with the law firm Hertz Schram PC, Bloomfield Hills, Michigan*

"The story of Nick Dubin is sadly becoming a more common occurrence. His experience as an individual with high functioning autism is one of being misunderstood and unfortunately undiagnosed until the age of twenty-seven. This book describes the compelling story of a young man caught up in a nightmare where his symptoms of autism and an uninformed criminal justice system collide. Attwood, Henault, Mr Dubin, and his parents offer a glimpse of a possible reality that, even though it is not commonly understood, many autistic teens and young adults have had to experience. Understanding societal rules for meeting others, for the development of interpersonal relationships, and sexuality in general are complex topics for any teen and young adult; it is especially complex for those on the autism spectrum. Proactive education is not only important, it is essential for those on the autism spectrum for without clear guidelines of what is right or wrong, what is allowed and what is illegal, and how to meet and express one's sexual feelings and needs, there will inevitably be more and more people on the autism spectrum finding themselves in the criminal justice system. This book is a brilliant first step or wake up call for individuals on the autism spectrum as well as their families."

> —*Lawrence R. Sutton, Ph.D., former Psychologist/Manager, Dept. of Public Welfare, Bureau of Autism, Western Region, State of Pennsylvania*

"As the father of a twenty-one-year-old son with autism and as a forensic psychologist who has been diagnosing sex offenders for forty years, I have an opinion on this subject. It is critical that high-functioning persons with autism read this book; and even more critical for the parents or guardians of persons with autism to read this book."

—*Michael C. Teague, Ph.D., former Raleigh Police Department Psychologist and former Chief of the Violent Crimes Section, North Carolina Department of Crime Control and Public Safety*

"Sexuality is among the most important issues in the field of ASD that no one is talking about. Well, finally that silence has been broken with an incredibly honest, moving, fascinating, and informative volume. The chapters by the family, whose son was charged with viewing child pornography, are among the most honest, gripping, and intense I have ever read and include a fantastic chapter by the son himself. In addition, there are two chapters written by renowned international experts in the field, which contain clear, comprehensive, and practical advice about sexuality related to people on the autism spectrum. Readers of this book will be rewarded with a whole new understanding of the major issues concerning sexuality and sexual development in ASD and will come away from this book deeply moved, surprised, and fully informed about the most important current issues in the field."

—*Gary B. Mesibov, Ph.D., Professor Emeritus, University of North Carolina*

"Rarely has a major challenge of national import to our law enforcement and legal systems been more eloquently expressed than through this courageous story of one remarkable young man, bewildered by his own entanglements. This book may not alleviate the suffering of many before him; but it should prevent the destruction of many lives of adults with Asperger's syndrome whose fragile balance act within a society they struggle to adjust to is violently shaken by a system too rigid to understand, too self-righteous to be just, and too unforgiving to consider facts and clinical knowledge. Mr Dubin, together with two of the foremost experts in the field, has given a powerful voice to a mission that belongs to us all: to correct an injustice that is still largely unknown but to the many families whose lives unravel at the strike of a sudden door knock."

—*Ami Klin, Ph.D., Marcus Autism Center, Children's Healthcare of Atlanta and Emory University School of Medicine*

"This courageous, insightful, and provocative book opens a timely and urgent discussion on a difficult topic, presenting multiple perspectives on an issue of enormous consequence. As a lawyer who has walked with clients and families through ordeals similar to this one, I'm grateful to Nick Dubin and his co-authors for illuminating an issue too often shrouded in secrecy and shame. This book should be of wide interest to those in law enforcement and the criminal justice system as well as clinicians, individuals with autism, and their families."

—*Lisa Greenman, Criminal Defense Attorney specializing in issues relating to developmental disability and mental health and Co-founder of Take-2, a summer program for children with autism, Washington, DC*

by the same authors

Asperger Syndrome and Anxiety
A Guide to Successful Stress Management
Nick Dubin
Foreword by Valerie Gaus
ISBN 978 1 84310 895 5
eISBN 978 1 84642 922 4

The Autism Spectrum and Depression
Nick Dubin
Foreword by Tony Attwood
ISBN 978 1 84905 814 8
eISBN 978 0 85700 242 6

The Complete Guide to Asperger's Syndrome
Tony Attwood
ISBN 978 1 84310 495 7 (hardback)
ISBN 978 1 84310 669 2 (paperback)
eISBN 978 1 84642 559 2

Asperger's Syndrome and Sexuality
From Adolescence through Adulthood
Isabelle Hénault
Foreword by Tony Attwood
ISBN 978 1 84310 189 5
eISBN 978 1 84642 235 5

THE AUTISM SPECTRUM, SEXUALITY AND THE LAW

What every parent and professional needs to know

Tony Attwood, Isabelle Hénault and Nick Dubin

Jessica Kingsley *Publishers*
London and Philadelphia

Authors' note

Some of the names have been changed in this book to protect the privacy
of the individuals involved.

Publisher's note

Larry and Kitty Dubin are available to speak to your group or organization.
If you are interested please contact our US office at hello.usa@jkp.com

First published in 2014
by Jessica Kingsley Publishers
73 Collier Street
London N1 9BE, UK
and
400 Market Street, Suite 400
Philadelphia, PA 19106, USA

www.jkp.com

Copyright © Tony Attwood, Isabelle Hénault and Nick Dubin 2014

Library of Congress Cataloging in Publication Data
A CIP catalog record for this book is available from the Library of Congress

British Library Cataloguing in Publication Data
A CIP catalogue record for this book is available from the British Library

ISBN 978 1 84905 919 0
eISBN 978 0 85700 679 0

Printed and bound in the United States

Contents

Introduction

Tony Attwood

Nick Dubin is an amazing young man. In this book, he has a story to tell of his experiences that will have a significant and beneficial effect on the understanding of autism spectrum disorders such as Asperger's syndrome and the degree of understanding and support needed throughout a person's life.

Nick did not choose to have Asperger's syndrome and throughout his childhood he had to adapt to having a different way of perceiving, thinking and relating in comparison with his peers. He has been determined that his experiences of adversity, many of which are harrowing to read, should be used constructively to improve our understanding of Asperger's syndrome and to develop support strategies so that others with the syndrome do not experience the same adversity, confusion and consequences.

Nick has a remarkably positive personality. I have great respect for his psychological resilience and the constructive way that he wants his experiences to be of benefit to others. He has considerable academic achievements, including a Master's degree in Learning Disabilities and a Doctorate in Psychology. He is the author of a series of excellent and highly recommended books on bullying, managing anxiety and coping with depression. All are based on his personal experiences and provide an eloquent insight into the world as perceived and experienced by someone who has Asperger's syndrome. His books provide practical strategies that can be used by teachers, parents and especially those who have Asperger's syndrome.

He is also a very honourable and brave young man, who is by nature extraordinarily sensitive, possessing commendable tenacity and altruism. How can such a person come into conflict with the criminal justice system and become a convicted felon and a registered sex offender? It is important that the reader now suspends any moral judgements and, with open-minded compassion, learns how Nick unwittingly violated the law and had to face the consequences. Then the reader and the community can learn from his experiences, so that others do not follow the same path. That is why this book has been published.

MY STORY

Nick Dubin

Preface

When I was around five or six years old, even though my family was Jewish, I sometimes went to Catholic mass with my babysitter and her mother. I would sit dutifully and listen to the priest deliver his sermon. On one occasion, he quoted the Apostle Paul who profoundly stated, "I die daily." As he recited this phrase, my young mind wondered how it was possible to die more than once in a lifetime, let alone more than once in the same week. Today, that statement fully resonates with me. Every day, I am living a dark night of the soul. Dying daily is the equivalent of what the Buddhists call an ego death. When someone undergoes an ego death, his or her old sense of self or identity dissolves, giving way to the birth of a more integrated or evolved self.

Since October 6, 2010, when I was arrested on charges of possessing child pornography, I have undergone an ego death. I know what it means to have one's entire sense of self stripped away in less than a heartbeat. In a single moment in time, I went from a respected member of the Asperger's community who had written several books, served on boards of directors, and spoken all over the country, to an alleged criminal facing prosecution by the United States of America in a federal court of law.

During the three years plus since my arrest, I have gained a much deeper understanding of myself through many hours of therapy and a great deal of soul searching. My goal has been an honest examination of why I viewed child pornography. Prior to my arrest, I lacked many insights that I have since acquired from this intense period of reflection. The results of this journey are expressed in the chapters that comprise my portion of this book. I admit I am reluctant to tell my story because I don't want people to misinterpret my motives. I want readers to understand the reasons why I have chosen to share this horrific experience.

First, I care deeply about the Asperger's community. Since being diagnosed with Asperger's syndrome in 2004, I have felt a deep kinship with this fine group of people. I've met hundreds of individuals on the autism spectrum and learned something important from each of them. I've sensed the pride many Aspies feel in their sense of uniqueness and I have shared that pride with them. From 2004 to 2010, I had written extensively on the strengths and potential that those with Asperger's struggle to actualize in their social, educational, and work lives. Out of an affinity and respect for this community, I am telling my story in an effort to highlight an issue that to date has not received sufficient attention. This issue is the correlation between the social deficits inherent in Asperger's and the subsequent impact these deficits can have on identity, interpersonal relationships, and sexuality. Although it seems obvious that having a delayed and/or impaired social development would significantly impact one's sexual development, this correlation has been largely ignored. To be clear, being on the spectrum doesn't mean a person will engage in illegal activities like viewing child pornography. At the same time, being on the autism spectrum does create certain vulnerabilities that can make a person susceptible to having social and sexual issues. My story is only about me, yet I believe there is much to be learned from my case.

I look forward to the contributions that my co-authors, Dr Tony Attwood and Dr Isabelle Hénault, will make to help fill in the gaps of this extremely important subject. I hope this information will not only be helpful to those with Asperger's, but also to their parents, teachers, mental health workers, and others who love and support them.

After my arrest, I received a number of letters from leaders in the Asperger's community offering their support and advice. Coming at the lowest point in my life, these letters meant the world to me.

They expressed encouragement and also the hope that sometime in the future I would be able to use this traumatic experience to help others. Over time, I have taken this message to heart. Needless to say, the prospect of talking about my social and sexual development is incredibly embarrassing and scary for me. I would have absolutely no desire to do this unless I was convinced that my contribution, along with my esteemed co-authors, would be helpful to the Asperger's population, as well as those who support them. In other words, my objective in participating in this book is to make a difference.

So, after months of going back and forth, I have decided to put aside my concerns for personal privacy and jump into the deep end of the pool. I believe sharing my experience will help me make things right. I want to know that when my time is up, I haven't left behind any unfinished business. If I have to sacrifice a considerable amount of pride and face the judgment of others for the good of a community that I care so deeply about, I believe it a worthwhile endeavor.

Before I begin, I need to clarify one very important point. Being charged with possession of child pornography is very different from being charged with a sexual contact offense. The idea of touching a child has never crossed my mind and the thought of doing so actually sickens me. It is important to cover this point for anyone who may be wondering if my behavior ever went beyond looking at images on my computer in the privacy of my residence. It did not. The prosecutors acknowledged that fact to be true.

So, with fear in my heart but an unwavering desire to shed light on an important issue, here is my story, which I hope will bring forth broader insights for the Asperger's and autism community.

CHAPTER 1

The Arrest

Like most people with Asperger's syndrome, I am extremely sensitive to noise. Every night I go to sleep with three sound machines blasting away (a waterfall, ocean waves, birds chirping), as well as a loud fan. The fan isn't on to keep me cool; it's to further amplify the roar of the sound machines and to preclude any outside noises from interfering with my sleep.

On October 6, 2010, as usual, I had the three sound machines and my loud fan on. At 6:30 a.m., I woke up to use the bathroom and noticed my dog, Sadie, walking around nervously. This was very unusual. She always slept quietly and didn't move from her dog bed the entire night. Sadie typically wouldn't wake up until I turned off at least two of the sound machines or the fan. But on this particular morning, she was pacing and acting strangely. I told her to get back in her bed.

I managed to fall back asleep but about fifteen minutes later Sadie's nervous pacing once again awakened me. Figuring that she probably had to go outside, I lay there trying to muster the energy to get out of bed to take her for a walk. Just at that moment, I heard a noise. It was loud enough to penetrate my cocoon of white noise. Then I heard another sound similar to the first. Big thumps, one after another. Was it possible that the elderly lady who lived in the apartment above mine was moving furniture at 6:30 a.m.? I dismissed that thought, as the sound didn't seem to be coming from above me. It seemed to be originating from outside my apartment. Maybe it was an earthquake? Not likely in Detroit. Half awake, I wondered if there was some kind of renovation going on in the hallways common to all the apartments in my building. But why would they be working so early in the morning? The sounds were getting louder and I was suddenly aware that they were actually coming closer to my apartment. My heart almost came out of my chest. What happened next turned out to be the most shocking and devastating experience of my life.

From my bed, I could see through the heating and cooling vent close to the top of the wall that there were bright lights flashing on and off in the hallway adjoining my bedroom. At this point, I wondered if there was some electrical problem with the lights in the hallway of my apartment. But that didn't explain all the loud noises. After rejecting all these different possibilities, the thought finally dawned on me: I had company. I wasn't sure who it could be but someone was breaking into my apartment.

I immediately thought I was going to die. I looked at Sadie and realized that this could be the last time I would ever see her. There was no time to reach for my cellphone to call the police and report a break-in or even call my mom and dad to say goodbye.

I could now tell that there was more than one person. Even though I couldn't make out any voices, I knew that one person wasn't capable of producing the cacophony of sounds that were being generated in the hallway leading to my apartment. The sounds were coming closer. The moment of confrontation I had been dreading for the last thirty seconds or so was now at hand. The intruders were coming in.

Suddenly, the door to my bedroom was forcibly pushed open and I heard someone shout, "Get out of bed. Get your hands up. Get 'em up, right now!" At least five men with flashlights all shining towards my face started coming towards me.

"What do you want?" I asked meekly.

"Out of bed right now! Get your hands up and spread 'em."

Even though I was wearing a T-shirt and sweatpants, I felt vulnerable and exposed as I got out of bed. "What's going on?" I asked. "Are you here just for me? Is something going on with the building? Is there a fire? Are you the fire department?"

"We're here for you. There's no fire. Now turn and face the wall. Don't resist."

The fact that I didn't faint and could actually speak was a miracle. I was scared out of my wits but my adrenaline was kicking in. My mind raced as to what I should do. If I tried to run away they would probably kill me but if I surrendered they might do the same thing. I realized that I had no options. I didn't even have time to think about Sadie.

"Why are you here?" I asked again.

"Just do what I tell you."

Suddenly, one of the men came towards me and pushed me against the wall. Then he put handcuffs on me. I could hardly breathe. "We'll tell you why we're here in a second. Remain still and don't move," he ordered.

Handcuffs? What was going on? Was I being arrested for something? That thought seemed even crazier than the idea of burglars breaking in and killing me. I still couldn't see anything because the room was dark and the flashlights were shining into my face. It felt as if the fires of hell were piercing my eyes with their bright intensity. For an Aspie, it was a sensory nightmare. I begged these men, "Please, tell me what's going on!"

"We'll tell you in a second. He's cuffed," one man said to the others in the room.

I was starting to think that these men were police because of the handcuffs. But that didn't make any sense to me. I was a law-abiding citizen who never smoked a cigarette, had a drink, or drove over the speed limit. I had even been called a "goody two shoes" more than a few times in my life. As one of the men checked to see that the handcuffs were firmly secured around my wrists, my denial was finally over. I realized I was being arrested for something. I just had no idea for what.

The next thing I remember I was being thrown on my living-room couch. Only a few minutes had passed from the time they barged into my bedroom to my being on the couch, but at the time it seemed like an eternity. Then, the lights in the living room were suddenly turned on and I saw about a dozen men surrounding me wearing FBI vests. I couldn't believe it. The FBI? The same group who hunts down dangerous criminals like Osama Bin Laden, Charles Manson, and the Mafia? The FBI broke into my apartment? And there weren't just one or two, but about a dozen of them. Before I could make sense out of what was happening, they were all moving throughout my apartment.

"Just tell me what's going on," I pleaded with one of the agents.

"I already told you that we'll explain what's happening when we're ready to do so."

"Clear," said one voice coming from my office where my computer was situated. "Clear," said another voice coming from my bedroom. "Clear," said another voice coming from my bathroom. I had no idea what "clear" meant in the context of what they were saying because I had never even seen an episode of *Law and Order*, *CSI*, *NCIS*, *Criminal Minds*, nor any other crime show. As a matter of fact, I had no interest in anything to do with criminal law.

"Why am I in handcuffs?" I asked, sweat pouring down my face.

"Clear," I heard again from another agent. The agent looked at his cohorts and apparently was given a silent all clear signal because he came over and removed the handcuffs. He then sat down on another couch in the living room, looked right at me, and said words I will never forget: "We're here to execute a search warrant." I was dumbstruck.

"A search warrant?" I asked timidly. Of course I knew what a search warrant was but I had no idea why they were searching *my* apartment.

"We've been granted by order of the court permission to enter your premises and search it."

"What? I'm confused," I replied, struggling to maintain my composure and trying not to have the biggest meltdown of my life.

The agent gave me a long, hard stare and then said very slowly and deliberately, "You want to tell us about something on your computer?"

At that moment, I felt my heart sink below my stomach. The only possibility that might have brought the FBI to my door was that I had looked at child pornography on my computer. But wait a minute. How did they know that? I had done that in the privacy of my apartment with no one else around. I wasn't even aware at the time why my actions would be considered so dangerous as to warrant about a dozen FBI agents breaking into my place and handcuffing me. I had never harmed anyone in my life. In fact, I was someone who had been victimized by bullies throughout my childhood.

When I looked at child pornography, I always experienced a sense of shame, which I didn't completely understand at that time. However, my shame didn't lead me to make the broader connection as to the illegality of this behavior. I had no idea that if you looked at child pornography the consequences would be that the FBI could break into your apartment, throw you against the wall, handcuff you, take away your computer, and charge you with a crime. Since my arrest, I have come to understand why viewing child pornography is illegal as well as why it is morally wrong. After I was arrested, my therapist explained to me that the children in the images I was viewing are victims and I feel great remorse for their degradation. Unfortunately, I was not able to make these connections prior to my arrest and I deeply regret my actions. My greatest sadness is wishing I knew then what I know now.

When the FBI agent began to question me, I responded with typical Asperger's honesty. "You're here because I have child pornography on my computer?"

He confirmed this by saying yes.

"How did you know this was on my computer? Was my computer being traced or something?"

He calmly replied, "That's not your concern. Is there anything else you want to tell us about what's on your computer?"

A few moments of silence passed. During that time, the other agents were still scattered about my apartment, going in and out of the different rooms. All this commotion was severely traumatizing. I always considered my apartment a sanctuary; a peaceful place where I could find solitude and be sheltered and protected from the outside world. This intrusion felt like an assault on my soul.

I finally summoned the nerve to ask the agent the question that was terrifying me. "Is this a serious crime?"

A small smile crossed his face. I wasn't sure why he smiled but in retrospect I think it meant I had asked a very stupid question. "It's very serious," he answered.

"How serious?" I asked, trembling with fear.

"Well, that depends on how cooperative you are. The more cooperative you are, the more it will help you." I had no idea what he meant.

"I'll do anything you want me to do," I pleaded. Later my lawyer told me that it is always best not to make any statements to authorities without a lawyer present. But at that time I was eager to please and wanted to be as cooperative as possible. I didn't realize the agents had failed to read me my Miranda rights even though I was vigorously questioned and in custody for four hours in my apartment.

"Am I under arrest?" I asked.

"Right now, you're not under arrest. We're executing the search warrant of your premises."

I decided to talk to the FBI agent as I had nothing to hide and hoped that, as he had reassured me, it would help my cause. The agent then asked me where I was employed. I told him I was a consultant to the faculty at a high school for students with Asperger's syndrome.

The fact that I had a job working at a school seemed to raise a red flag. I explained that I had Asperger's syndrome myself and that was the main reason I had been hired for this job. He then made reference to my previous work at a social service agency where many children came for help.

"How do you explain that?" he asked accusingly. I was shocked the FBI was aware of my past employment. I told the agent that when I worked at this agency, I only worked with adults and explained that my job primarily consisted of assisting adult groups and giving presentations to the public on various subjects related to autism. The FBI also knew I had been a tennis instructor for a number of years and assumed I had worked with children in that capacity, which was true. I explained that when I was in high school I had been offered a job teaching tennis at a local country club because I had been one of the best junior tennis players in the area. From 1995 to 2004, I had taught at a variety of tennis clubs. Because of all the social demands involved with these jobs, I never enjoyed being a tennis instructor, even though I took my work very seriously.

The agent then asked who my boss was at my current place of employment. I told him the name of the headmaster of the school. He informed me that they would be visiting the school in the next day or two. Enormous waves of guilt immediately passed through me. The school where I worked was in its first year, trying to establish itself as a premier academy for high-school students with Asperger's. I was quite proud of what my boss had been able to achieve and feared I would cause the school negative publicity. I begged them not to go to the school but those pleas were ignored. In hindsight, I now understand they were just doing their job. They had to investigate whether any improprieties took place while I had worked there.

During the course of the interrogation, I learned that not only was I being charged with possession of child pornography, but also for distribution of this material, an even more serious offense. That made no sense at all, as I had never distributed this material to anyone else. I subsequently learned from my lawyer that once these images are downloaded, a file is created on the computer that acts as a Trojan horse and becomes automatically accessible to other people, including the FBI. You don't have to intentionally send these images to someone else for another person to be able to receive them. So even though I never intended to distribute this material to anyone, under law, the government still considered it to be an act of distribution. I later learned this is a common practice that explains how the FBI is able to gain knowledge that a person, acting in privacy, is downloading child pornography at no charge on his or her computer. Because I lacked this basic understanding, I was now facing a mandatory five-year minimum prison sentence under a federal statute in addition to a possible prison term for possession of child pornography.

It was now 10:00 a.m. and the agents were still interrogating me and searching my apartment. They went through every nook and cranny of my unit and even threatened to get a warrant to search my car unless I gave a signed consent on the spot. Thinking they would stay all day waiting for the warrant to be approved, and desperate for them to leave, I gave them a signed consent allowing them to search my car.

The FBI had now been there for close to four hours. They saw I was visibly weak and asked if I had any medical problems or history. I told them I had diabetes and was taking antidepressants for depression. Before they left, they wanted to call someone to come over because they could see I was in a very distressed state. I gave them permission to call my father.

My father was driving to work that morning when he received the call from the FBI agent. He was halfway to downtown Detroit when he heard what had happened. He immediately turned around and headed for my place, canceling his night and day classes at the law school where he has been a professor for the past three decades. He later told me that he missed several turns and even headed in the wrong direction at one point because he was so upset and distracted. I couldn't have possibly imagined at that moment what my dad must have been going through physically and emotionally. All I could think about was that I badly wanted him to be by my side. I wanted him there so I could hug him and be assured that he still loved me.

He finally arrived. I could smell the familiar scent of his cologne but I was too ashamed to look at him. After a few moments, I managed to turn my head slightly towards him and he came over and gave me the hug I had been longing for. I said, "Dad, I am so sorry."

He whispered "I love you" in my ear and then put his finger to his lips as if to say, "Not now, Nick." Before the FBI agents left, they told me I would be arraigned in federal court the next day. What I didn't know was that the arraignment would be in front of a packed courtroom with many media outlets present.

With the FBI finally gone, I started sobbing and hugging my dad as if I were a toddler who had been lost in a department store and had just been reunited with his father. I apologized over and over again for being such a bad son. He remained stoic, insisting I wasn't a bad son and that in fact I was a great son, but that right now we needed to go into action mode. The first two things he said that had to be done were to secure legal counsel and to make contact with the headmaster before the FBI visited the school. After the trauma of what I had just gone through, I knew I wouldn't be able to call my boss.

"Dad, I can't talk to him. I can't tell him what happened. It's too humiliating," I said.

"Well, you're going to have to resign," he said.

"I know that. Would you please resign for me?"

"Okay, let me go outside and I'll call him."

My heart was pounding like a drum as I waited for my dad to come back in and tell me how angry my boss was. Instead, my dad returned about twenty minutes later and told me something that brought me to my knees.

"I just had one of the most amazing conversations of my entire life," he said.

"What do you mean?"

"Well, your boss wants you to know that in the short time you were there, you made a great contribution to the school and he thinks you are a wonderful human being."

"Wait a minute. Didn't you tell him what happened?"

"I did. I explained what you're being charged with and that the FBI would be coming to the school. But he knows you, Nick. He understands who you are and respects you very much."

I was stunned. I fell to the floor and cried and cried until I had no more tears left. I cried because I felt the headmaster's words were like the grace of God cleansing my soul. I felt totally undeserving of his respect after potentially humiliating him and the school he had worked so hard to create. I couldn't believe it, but in the midst of this ugly situation, he showed that he cared about me. Understandably, once the FBI visited him, he was forced to accept my resignation. I am ever grateful for his belief that, in spite of the charges against me, he still saw me as a good person.

So, how did I get into this horrible predicament? How did I go from a person whose life had meaning and purpose to someone who was facing serious felony counts and could potentially spend years in prison? To understand what led up to this tragic event, I need to go back in time and trace my social and sexual development, within an Asperger's framework, starting in early childhood.

CHAPTER 2

Emerging Differences in Childhood

I was an only child, who grew up in an extremely loving family with two remarkably devoted parents. They both followed somewhat unconventional career paths, which I believe had an impact in shaping my future career. Dad is a law professor and a documentary filmmaker and Mom is a professional playwright who also teaches playwriting at a university. They waited until their thirties to have a child, so they were definitely ready to be parents. Dad liked to document every move I made. After I was born, he took a picture of me every day for quite a while, and later made a video of my first few years, complete with background music. When Mom held me in her arms for the first time in the hospital, the song he chose to underscore the moment was Marvin Gaye's "Pride and Joy."

We frequently visited my mother's family in Cleveland. I always looked forward to seeing my great-aunt Bertha, an eccentric and energetic woman who would do anything I asked. Even though she was in her seventies, if I said I wanted to ride up and down an elevator twenty times in a row, she was up for it. If I wanted her to blow bubbles with me for a couple of hours, that was fine with her too. I often slept at her house, which was always a treat. Before she put me to bed, she would read me a story of my choice and then massage my back while singing "Yankee Doodle Dandy."

Unlike my great-aunt, my grandmother was not that interested in playing with kids, but my grandfather more than made up for it. He was very outgoing and childlike at heart. He used to put me on the back of his motor scooter and we would ride around the block, waving and saying "Hi" to all his neighbors. He would take me sledding and play wiffle ball with me, and when I was older, he introduced me to tennis, which became a lifelong passion for me. My connection with him was strong.

I remember being happy as a toddler and unaware that problems were starting to arise in my development. My parents were becoming increasingly concerned that my speech was delayed and that I was exhibiting some unusual behaviors. When I was around three, my parents often took me to a local park. I enjoyed going down the slide and loved the repetition of that activity, that is, until some other child came along who also wanted to go down the slide. As far as I was concerned that was *my* slide and these other children were trespassers. When I was at the top of the slide ready to go down and another child climbed up the ladder behind me, I would have a major meltdown. I would yell at these other children to get off the slide and go away, having no clue that my behavior was inappropriate. Very embarrassed, my parents would grab me and make a hasty retreat, with me still screaming at the top of my lungs.

Another worrisome behavior I exhibited was touching people's heads. I would do this very lightly, not in an aggressive way. When I was three or four, this behavior was somewhat tolerated, but as I was exposed to more children in social and school situations, it became clear that it was annoying and I was reprimanded and scolded for it. At that time, no one understood I was doing this out of a need for tactile stimulation.

My intense motor activity was also different from other children my age. I would constantly jump up and down and flap my arms. My dad thought this behavior was cute and that I was just a highly energetic child, but my mother was very concerned about it. My parents were unaware that this kind of behavior is typical of an autistic child who is craving some form of physical stimulation and an outlet for release.

My parents were also troubled by a number of unusual fears I had. The sounds of the vacuum cleaner and the washing machine were particularly frightening to me. My mom says it got to the point where she had to wait until I was out of the house to use either one. I also had a fear of going down the drain in the bathtub. My parents tried every way they could to coax me into taking a bath but I really thought I would be lost for all eternity once they let the bathwater out. I am happy to say that eventually I got over this phobia.

Another strange fear was that I would become panic stricken when the music on a record player came to an end and the needle got stuck in the groove on the record. For some reason, the fact that the music had stopped playing but the record was still spinning around was confusing and scary to me and usually triggered a meltdown where I would start screaming at the top of my lungs.

In addition to these fears, I also began to develop some unusual special interests. Instead of playing with He-Man or Lego® like most boys my age, my favorite activity was watching television game shows. I especially liked *The $25,000 Pyramid*, *The Price is Right*, and *Card Sharks*. I particularly enjoyed listening to the hosts of these shows and memorized all their catchphrases and tried to talk like them to anyone who would listen. I also developed a fascination with maps and liked to figure out where different roads began and ended. Whenever my family would go on a road trip, I would throw a tantrum if my parents deviated in the slightest from the route I had decided we should take. It never occurred to me at that time that any of my interests were unusual or different from other children my age.

Although my parents were concerned about much of my development, their biggest worry was my speech delay. As a three-year-old, I had a very limited vocabulary, I couldn't form a sentence, and it was clear that I didn't understand much of what was being said to me. If someone asked me a question, I would just repeat the question instead of responding appropriately. This type of repetition is known as echolalia and is a red flag that the child does not comprehend what is being said.

In 1980, my pediatrician urged my parents to take me to have a developmental evaluation, which was offered by the school district where we lived. This was the first time I was ever in a formal educational setting outside my home and I was very uncooperative with the tester. The psychologist who tested me recommended that I immediately begin intensive speech therapy and be placed in a pre-primary kindergarten program for children with developmental disabilities the following fall. There was no mention of the word autism and, of course, Asperger's syndrome didn't exist as a diagnosis until 1994. Until I was properly diagnosed in 2004 at the age of twenty-seven, my parents and I remained confused and frustrated by my differences.

I went to a nearby hospital for speech therapy, where I was diagnosed with severe expressive and receptive language delays (aphasia). I met with Carol, the speech therapist, three times a week. I would sit on the floor directly across from her and she would repeatedly show me pictures that she wanted me to identify, such as a cup or a loaf of bread. This type of rote therapy would be referred to today as Applied Behavioral Analysis. Carol had a no-nonsense presence. If I started to get restless or wiggle around, she would say in a commanding voice, "Show me good sitting," and I would sit as still as a statue. If I did a good job that day, she would reward me with mini marshmallows at the end of the session. I liked going to the hospital and meeting with her. At age three, I didn't realize I was seeing her because my development was different or delayed. Carol was like a family member or a fun babysitter. In other words, I had no sense of being different.

With Carol's help, my speech improved dramatically over the summer. She said she had never seen a child with my deficits make this kind of progress over a three-month period and saw it as proof that I was gifted. My special education pre-kindergarten teacher, who I had met the previous spring, was also amazed. When I saw her again in the fall she called it a summer miracle because I had almost no language when we first met in the spring and now I was talking in complete sentences.

In spite of my progress, the next year when it came time for kindergarten, my parents recognized I was not ready to be mainstreamed so they enrolled me in two different schools. In the morning, I went to a private school with a ratio of ten students to three teachers. In the afternoon, a little yellow school bus would pick me up at home and take me to the public school's pre-kindergarten impaired program that was separate from the general education population. At this school, the ratio was three students to two teachers.

Although the teachers at both schools were sensitive to my needs, my poor fine motor skills made most of what was expected of me a torture. I wasn't able to perform simple tasks, like cutting, pasting, and drawing, that I could see the other children in my private school class could easily accomplish. Learning to print was a nightmare. I would clutch the pencil tightly in my fist, which produced totally illegible handwriting. Looking around and seeing my classmates do so many things I couldn't do was beginning to make me feel different.

My parents sensed my frustration and tried to help me find a creative outlet that better suited my interests and skills. My mom encouraged me to create stories. Because of my problems with handwriting, she suggested I dictate these stories to her and she would type them on the typewriter (this was before computers were household items). One day, I wrote a play called "How to Make Friends" where all of the characters were animals. As I recall, there was a hippo, a lion, an elephant, a crocodile, and a skunk. Strangely enough, it was the character of the skunk that ended up teaching everyone else the meaning of friendship. It is ironic that this little play foreshadowed what would turn out to be true for me later in life: that when I tried making friends with other children, I often felt like a skunk and that my greatest friends in life would turn out to be animals. More specifically, dogs.

Both my kindergarten classes were safe and sheltered environments, but first grade was just around the corner and my parents had a big decision to make. Should I be mainstreamed in the public school or be placed in a school for children with special needs? Carol, my speech therapist, encouraged my parents to send me to a school for gifted children because my language was now above average and she believed this type of environment would be best for my temperament. After my parents submitted an application to a school for gifted children, I had to go there for an interview so the teachers could evaluate how I interacted with other children.

I remember my dad dropping me off that day and telling me, "You're going to meet some nice kids this morning. Just relax and have fun." I knew my parents wanted the interview to go well. They didn't think I could handle public school and there wasn't a school for special needs that was appropriate for me at that time. I didn't want to disappoint them, but I could never have foreseen that my old nemesis, the record player, would be my Achilles heel. Unfortunately, at age seven, I still hadn't outgrown this strange fear.

I walked into the classroom and, seeing a group of other children, felt overwhelmed. A record player immediately caught my eye. Remembering what my dad had told me, I tried to play with some of the other kids. All seemed to go well for a while but when the music on the record player came to an end and I looked over and saw the needle still going around with no sound coming out, I had a full-fledged meltdown. The teachers were completely baffled by my inappropriate behavior and told my parents that this school was definitely not the right fit for me.

My mom and dad were now caught in a trap. They had major reservations about mainstreaming me but there were no other options available. This problem is common for Asperger's children and their parents. In fact, my mom and I recently watched an episode of the television show, *Parenthood*, where parents of a child with Asperger's were faced with the exact same dilemma. There is often no right school for Asperger's children and parents are understandably afraid to switch their child from the safety of a private or special needs school to the chaos and unpredictability of public school.

As it turned out, my parents' fears were not unfounded. First grade in the public school system was a total culture shock for me. I was used to being in warm, nurturing classrooms with a high student-teacher ratio, but all of a sudden I was one of twenty-eight children with only one unfriendly teacher. Looking back, my thirty-seven-year-old self feels great compassion for the harsh and abrupt transition my seven-year-old self had to make. I felt I had gone from paradise in early childhood, where I got a lot of love, attention, and praise, to the intense confusion of public school where I often felt disliked by my teachers and different from my peers.

In spite of all the early intervention I received before first grade, I never thought I was abnormal in any way. I thought everyone went to speech therapy three days a week, attended two different schools every day, and received occupational therapy. In first grade, I was suddenly being plucked out of class every day to go to a smaller classroom called the Learning Resource Center (LRC) with one teacher and just a few other students. Being in the LRC felt like kindergarten all over again, except that I was starting to figure out that something was wrong with me. Being the only one in my first grade classroom who had to leave every day to go to the LRC at a specific time put my differences on display for all to see. I hated my special education classes and continued to protest against going to them from first grade through my senior year in high school.

My first grade teacher was completely different from all the other teachers I previously had. She was tired and listless, with no energy or patience for a student with special needs. Whereas I was used to getting a lot of praise, she seemed generally irritated by me. Only weeks after school started, she told my parents I wasn't adjusting well to public school and was concerned about my lack of socializing, poor fine motor skills, and inability to pay attention.

One day in class, a bee flew in through the window and was buzzing around me. Terrified, I leapt out of my seat, started to scream, and ran around the room frantically trying to get away from the bee. The teacher tried assuring me that if I just remained still, the bee wouldn't bother me, but nothing she said would calm me down. That incident convinced her that I didn't belong in her class. The next day she told my mom that perhaps I belonged in a self-contained classroom. After my mom pleaded with her, she agreed to give me another chance. I managed to stay in her classroom for the rest of the year.

My second grade teacher was an elderly woman on the verge of retirement. She made Cruella De Vil seem warm and fuzzy. Academic demands were becoming overwhelming and any task requiring fine motor skills was still beyond me. Social difficulties were increasingly more visible. I was not playing well with other children and I couldn't understand why no one wanted to play with me. One day at lunch a girl said bluntly, "I don't like you. You're weird. Don't sit next to me." Other children weren't the only ones who lacked sensitivity. My art teacher held up one of my drawings in front of my classmates as an example of how not to do the assignment. Everyone laughed when they saw my picture, which looked as if it had been drawn by a two-year-old. I was embarrassed and ashamed. As painful as that was, another teacher humiliated me even more that year.

One day I was in the LRC and the teacher asked me and a classmate, Meghan, to go to Mrs Miller's room to get a student who was late for his scheduled time in the LRC. When Meghan and I got there, I tried opening the door but it was locked. I knocked on the door and said, "I can't open the door."

"What do you mean you can't open the door?" Mrs Miller asked incredulously.

"It's stuck. I can't open it." I replied.

"That's nonsense," she said, opening the door herself, and then immediately closing it. "Now Meghan, *you* open the door," she said.

I was relieved. I figured Meghan wouldn't be able to open the door either, which would prove there was something wrong with the door. But Meghan had no problem and Mrs Miller insisted I try to open the door again. For the life of me, it wouldn't budge. I just couldn't understand that a doorknob could be turned counterclockwise but evidently other second-graders could. While I struggled publicly with this mortifying lesson in door physics, I could hear the kids in Mrs Miller's class laughing at me.

"You mean to tell me that you're in second grade and you can't even open a door? What's wrong with you?" Mrs Miller asked rhetorically. Her harsh words brought me to tears and I ran away, disgusted with myself, wishing I could go home and never return.

Socially speaking, things outside of school were a little better for me. My mom regularly arranged play dates, and being at home with only one other child was a lot easier than being in the playground with twenty-seven classmates. My mom would encourage me (though it felt more like pressure at the time) to call a classmate to come over and play but the prospect of doing that terrified me. I would nervously pace in front of the phone for long periods of time, sometimes practicing what I should say, but in the end I always gave up.

My life improved dramatically in third grade because I had a wonderful teacher that year. She was warm, bubbly, and fresh out of college. She reminded me of the type of caring teachers I had before entering public school. Even though she had twenty-five other students, she went out of her way to connect with me. Sensing I was struggling socially, she paired me up with two other boys, Chris and Jack, who actually lived in my neighborhood. These boys became my first and only friends in the twelve years I attended public school. We shared an interest in the Detroit Pistons and The Beatles. My parents took these boys on family trips and I carpooled with them to school every day. When my dad drove us to school, he was always bothered that I would make him put the hard rock music station on the radio because that was the kind of music Chris and Jack liked. He knew that I didn't like it but I wanted them to think I did.

Of the two boys, Chris was the nicer one and Jack was more of a troublemaker. We always hung out at my house. I was seldom invited to either Chris's or Jack's home but I never questioned that. It just felt great to finally have friends and that made the rest of elementary school a lot better for me.

Things seemed to be going well. However, one day towards the end of fifth grade, a traumatic event occurred that is uncomfortable for me to talk about to this day. On the way home from school, Chris, Jack, and I went to play in the park, which was directly behind my house. Jack, who was the leader of the threesome and always called the shots said, "Hey, Nick, get on the swing and we can play cops and robbers."

"Okay," I said eagerly. I went over to the swing and before I knew what hit me, Jack had handcuffed me to the swing. Thinking that this was part of the game, I didn't panic at first but then Jack started laughing.

"We got him! C'mon, let's go," he said to Chris. Then they got on their bikes. "Loser," they yelled. "Sucker," Jack said.

I felt stupid that I fell for their prank and humiliated that this was happening in a public place. I wondered if there was something I did to make them angry with me. After all the time we spent together, how could they do this to me?

I pleaded with them to take the handcuffs off, but they just kept taunting me. The longer this went on, the more frightened I became. I started screaming for help.

Moments later, my dad appeared in the backyard to see what all the yelling was about. To his horror, he saw me handcuffed to a swing with Chris and Jack on their bikes circling me. As soon as they saw my dad, they immediately came over and removed the handcuffs.

Jack whispered to me, "Tell your dad we were just playing cops and robbers. You wouldn't rat on a friend. We wouldn't do that to you." Chris just looked down at the ground.

"Dad," I said, holding back tears. "Everything's all right. We were just playing a game."

"It didn't sound like a game to me," he said.

"No, that's all it was. I'm fine." I reassured him.

After they left, I told my dad the truth. He knew how much my friends meant to me, but he had to address this incident for my own personal safety. The next day they showed up at my house as if nothing had happened. I told my dad not to say anything, but he was determined to set them straight. He was controlled but there was no mistaking his anger.

"What you did to Nick yesterday was not only unacceptable, it was cruel," he said to Chris and Jack. "You cannot treat him that way. You're still welcome here but not if you're going to act this way."

That was all he said but it was the end of the friendship. I was furious at him for causing me to lose my only friends and I couldn't forgive him for a long time.

Unfortunately, this incident had a lasting impact on me. It took me years to realize that Chris and Jack were never really my friends. I was just so grateful to have them to play with that I was willing to put up with the inequality of the relationship. I never suspected Jack could do something like that to me and was even more upset with Chris, whom I really liked and trusted. For a long time this experience made it difficult for me to trust anyone to be my friend.

Elementary school was now coming to an end and the transition to middle school was just ahead of me. Transitions are hard for everyone, but they are especially difficult for those with Asperger's. Going from private to public school had been a major challenge for me. Although I had some good years, it was during this time that I started to see myself as different from my peers. In a few months, I would be starting middle school where I would discover just how different I really was.

CHAPTER 3

Middle School

Years of Confusion

Adolescence creates feelings of confusion for virtually everyone. This confusion is intensified in someone who feels much younger than his chronological age and is also coping with the emergence of sexual feelings. As an adolescent with Asperger's, this is exactly how I felt in middle school.

Although I wasn't aware of it, during the first few weeks of middle school my guidance counselor was observing me from a distance in different areas of the school—the classroom, the cafeteria, the gym. The counselor could see how isolated I was in these settings and was concerned about my social adjustment to middle school. One day she asked me to come to her office to discuss what was going on with me.

"You seem to be having a hard time so far. Is there anything I can do to make things easier?" she inquired.

My reply surprised her. "Actually there is something. Is there any way I can go back to elementary school?" I wasn't being sarcastic or trying to make a joke. I was dead serious.

She looked stunned. "When you say 'go back' do you mean to visit your old teachers from time to time?"

"No, I want to go back and be a student there instead of here."

"Well, I'm sorry, honey, but that's not possible," she replied. "What's wrong with middle school? Why do you want to go back to elementary school?"

"Because I don't like it here at all," I said. "Things are too confusing."

"Confusing in what way?" she asked.

"I don't really know. I just know I don't like it here. Please let me go back to elementary school."

From my point of view, this request wasn't unreasonable. Middle school was much too complicated for me and I longed to return to the simplicity of elementary school. I missed having one teacher instead of seven. I missed being with the same group of students all day. I missed staying in the same classroom instead of having to travel to different rooms with only four minutes in between classes to get what I needed from my locker. Everything was so different from what I was used to and the changes felt overwhelming. It was the same way I felt when I started first grade in public school, but now I felt even more lost and unprepared entering middle school.

Shortly after my discussion with the guidance counselor, she called my parents. She told them I wanted to go back to elementary school and that she was concerned about how socially isolated I was. She recommended a therapy group, outside of school, for adolescents who were struggling socially and finding middle school an alienating experience. My parents agreed to meet with the therapist who ran the group. Knowing me as well as they did, they told the therapist that it was highly unlikely I would be willing to attend such a group. The therapist told my mom and dad they needed to take parental responsibility and, in essence, force me to go to the group, even if I resisted. She said that *they* were in charge and should not let me run the show. She pointed out that the group was in my best interest and that all the other kids in the group really liked it.

My parents came up with what they thought was a clever strategy. They said I only had to attend one session and if I didn't like it, I didn't have to go back. They described the group as if it were an after-school social group, rather than a therapeutic outlet for social misfits. I can't believe my parents thought that if I went to this group once I would want to attend on a regular basis, but apparently they were counting on it.

Against my better judgment, I agreed to attend one session and one session only. I'm sure what happened next will come as no surprise. When I walked into the first session, I was immediately horrified to see that the group was nothing like my parents' description. The kids were all clearly social outcasts and the therapist actually expected us to talk about our problems and feelings. There was no way in hell I was going to spend time with these nerds who were the opposite of the cool kids at school I desperately wanted to be like. So, after the first session, I called my parents' bluff and told them I wanted out. My parents, feeling the pressure of not letting me run the show, reneged on their promise to let me decide if I wanted to leave the group and insisted that I keep going. To say I was outraged is a colossal understatement.

The next week when my dad dropped me off for the second session, I really let him have it. "You lied to me. You told me if I didn't like the group, I wouldn't have to go back. I'll never forgive you as long as I live."

The ensuing power struggles between my parents and me over whether or not I would attend this group continued every week throughout most of middle school. But in my mind, my mom and dad weren't the real problem. The therapist was. She had completely brainwashed my parents. Until she gave them the sign that I was ready to "graduate," I had to remain in the group. Because she exercised so much control over my parents, she held all the cards and I deeply resented her for it. As a result, I tried everything I could to alienate her so she would want to get rid of me sooner rather than later. I didn't talk to other members of the group, I was unresponsive when she asked me anything, and I even insulted her once by comparing her to Saddam Hussein. None of my strategies worked. In fact, they worked against me. The therapist wasn't fazed by my behavior and she convinced my parents that the more I resisted being in the group, the more I needed to be there. Although I can't imagine why, the therapist finally released me from the group.

I believe this titanic struggle between my parents and me could have been avoided if I had understood that being different wasn't necessarily a bad thing and could even be considered an asset. But at the time I didn't want to be different. I wanted to fit in. I wanted friends and I was afraid that if someone at school found out that I was in this group everyone would officially know I was different. The joke was on me. Everyone at school already knew I was different. I was being unnecessarily paranoid and wouldn't connect with other kids in the group, some of whom, like me, had probably not yet been diagnosed with Asperger's syndrome. Maybe if, at the time, I had understood that I had a social disability, I would have made a friend or two, which was all I really wanted in the first place. It was definitely my loss—a result of sheer stubbornness and lack of understanding.

Not surprisingly, being in the group had little to no effect on my social isolation at school. At lunchtime I would pace the periphery of the cafeteria but never sit down at a table with other kids. One reason I had trouble socializing was my lack of interest in pop culture. I didn't like what the other kids were always talking about, such as Guns N' Roses, *Star Wars*, and *Beverly Hills, 90210*. All I had to bring to the table were my special interests and, unfortunately, game shows, maps, and the music of Frank Sinatra were of no appeal to my peers. One day in sixth grade science class I was humming a Sinatra tune quietly to myself. One of the boys who regularly bullied me asked me to sing the song out loud. Not understanding that he was setting me up for ridicule, I started singing "Night and Day," trying to sound like Ol' Blue Eyes, and everyone started to laugh. I interpreted this laughter as a positive response. At least it was some form of attention and I wasn't being ignored.

Every day my mom would pack me a brown bag lunch, which I always tossed into the garbage. I intentionally gave my parents the impression that I ate lunch with other kids rather than tell them I was always alone and threw away my food. Skipping lunch meant that I didn't eat all day, which was not only an unhealthy habit but reduced my already limited ability to concentrate.

During free time at lunch, I would sometimes venture into the gym where kids were playing basketball. They would either be playing full court games or simply shooting baskets. One day, I picked up a basketball and started shooting from just beyond the three-point line. First ball, swish. Second ball, swish. Third ball, swish. Before I knew it, I had made about ten three pointers in a row. This was amazing because I wasn't very good at basketball. I couldn't dribble well, I had no blocking ability, and my layups were off the mark. But when it came to shooting three pointers, I discovered that I had an almost savant-like knack for being able to make a series of three-point shots. Shooting three pointers became a skill I loved showing off to my peers at lunch because it earned me some attention and a bit of notoriety. Several years ago, I heard about an autistic teen in upstate New York who made international headlines by sinking six, three pointers in a row during a high school game. It brought back memories of me in sixth grade and made me smile.

Around this time, my parents began to put pressure on me to socialize. For example, they wanted me to attend school football games where I would sit alone in the bleachers and feel like a total loser. Then they asked me to do the unthinkable—go to a school dance. This was an utterly terrifying prospect for a couple of reasons. First, I didn't know how to dance and second, I didn't know any girls who I thought would want to dance with me. I refused to go but after several fights I finally gave in just to get my parents off my back. I wound up going to the dance alone and felt totally unprepared for what awaited me. As I stood on the sidelines of the gym watching all the other kids, it seemed as if everyone was having a good time but me. The bright swirling lights and the deafening music created a sensory overload for me. I didn't talk to a single person the whole night and left the dance feeling as if I was an alien from a far distant planet. I dreaded coming home and having my parents ask me, "Did you have a good time?"

I wasn't having much contact with girls, but my contact with some of the boys at school was quite negative. They were starting to call me gay. This was very confusing to me. Did this mean I was gay? Was I doing something effeminate that I wasn't aware of? Perhaps if I had known I had Asperger's at the time, this situation would have made more sense to me. Many teens on the autism spectrum are called gay by their peers when most of the time they are not gay. They are often perceived this way because their psychosexual development is delayed and they have not yet begun interacting with the opposite sex. Teenagers frequently use the word gay as a synonym for stupid or weird, having nothing to do with homosexuality, but that is not how I interpreted the use of the word at the time. Unfortunately, being called gay can cause great confusion and shame for an Asperger's adolescent, as it did for me.

I was also confused because I didn't have any crushes on girls. I knew that this was not the way things should be progressing and wondered if my lack of interest was due to my social immaturity. Did I not like girls because I was simply not ready to like girls or could there be some other explanation?

Not being attracted to girls bothered me, but even more troubling was that I felt attracted to some same-sex classmates. This didn't make any sense to me. On top of that, the classmates to whom I felt attracted were actually some of the same boys who were bullying me. How could that be? Was what I was feeling something I would eventually grow out of or was I—dare I say it—gay? This thought was completely unacceptable to me. I couldn't be gay. I had more than enough things wrong or different about me. Why add one more thing?

To prove that I was just like my male peers, I tried convincing them that I also liked girls. For example, I bought a *Playboy* magazine from a classmate for ten dollars. My reasoning was that if he thought I was looking at *Playboy*, he would have no doubt about my sexuality. I also used to tell certain boys about crushes I had on various girls in school and went into a lot of detail so my stories would sound credible.

Unfortunately, these efforts on my part didn't have the desired effect. As sixth grade went on, the bullying escalated and some very troubling incidents took place in the boys' locker room. One time as I was undressing for swimming, a classmate stole my shorts and underpants. He then threw my clothes over to another boy and they began to toss them back and forth. Standing there stark naked, I was embarrassed and terrified. But I wasn't just terrified about what these boys were doing to me. I was terrified by the possibility of becoming aroused without my underwear on.

"Doobies got them boobies, he sucks them at the movies," said one of the boys. Soon others in the locker room chimed in and a chant began. Their words pierced my heart like small daggers. In the meantime, my underwear and shorts were being thrown from boy to boy while I tried desperately to get them back.

There were other times in the locker room when the same boys who snatched my clothes pretended to come on to me. They'd say things like, "You know you want it, Dubin. C'mon, just touch it. You're horny for me, aren't you?" These boys would also expose themselves to me in an attempt to try to get me to touch them.

I never knew when this game of keep away was going to happen and whenever I went into the locker room I was terrified this could be the next time. These recurring incidents caused me to suffer much emotional distress during my middle school years. I blocked out these shameful experiences for many years and only recently relived them in therapy with the benefit of clarity and insight from my therapist.

Coping with this kind of abuse was draining and left me little energy for schoolwork. Consequently, my intellectual curiosity vanished and didn't return until my freshman year of college. Somehow I managed to get mostly Cs; considering my lack of effort this was quite an accomplishment. Needless to say, my mom and dad weren't pleased when progress reports were mailed home and it was evident how my grades were suffering. During middle school, my only objective was survival. After spending seven hours most days being humiliated by my peers as well as criticized by my teachers, I would go home and try to decompress and not think about school again until the next day.

Being in special education classes in middle school was even more embarrassing than it was in elementary school. I simply didn't want others to know that I got this extra support for math and science and help with organizational skills. I didn't want to be viewed as stupid or different. So I would wait until the very last minute, right before the bell rang and the other students were already in their next class, before I entered the Learning Resource Center.

It should come as no surprise that I began to experience signs of clinical depression in middle school. I felt sad and hopeless and had occasional suicidal thoughts, which I never acted upon. The idea of suicide was tempting because I figured a quick end to things would be much easier than nine months a year of torture and anguish. Every day on my way home from school, I passed a bridge that hung over the railroad tracks. In my mind, that bridge was a place I could go to if I ever decided I couldn't take it any longer.

Life at home was also difficult in middle school. Typically, my pattern was to hold in all the anger, rage, and shame I experienced at school until the moment I stepped inside my house. Sadly, my parents became the target of all those pent up feelings. I constantly yelled and screamed at them. Who else could I yell and scream at? This behavior created a tremendous amount of tension and strain in our family life and is something I deeply regret as an adult. My parents didn't deserve that anger directed at them, but at the time they were my only outlet. I suppose another option would have been to turn all that rage against myself. Because my parents absorbed much of my anger, they might have unwittingly helped save my life.

Feeling like a failure in almost every aspect of my life, I turned my attention towards my special interests, which were always a good distraction. My fascination with game shows continued and watching televangelists also mesmerized me. This was strange considering I came from a humanistic Jewish background. Observing closely how these charismatic men delivered their sermons, I developed a routine known as "the preacher" where I combined several of these men into one impersonation. I performed this routine once at school and it caught on instantly. Every day, kids would come up to me and demanded that I do the preacher. A crowd would gather around me. I loved the attention and hearing everyone laugh.

After a while, all this attention turned into a constant demand for me to do my routine. Kids would say that if I didn't do the preacher they'd steal my lunch money or strip me in the locker room. Even though I had grown tired of doing the preacher, I usually gave in. I guess I was enjoying the attention. It took me a while to finally realize that kids were laughing *at* me, not *with* me. What should have been a clue was that the same kids who wanted me to do the preacher were often the same ones who harassed me in the locker room.

In an effort to get some of the bullies to leave me alone, I started to give away money. I used my special interest in game shows as part of my master plan. I asked these boys if they wanted to participate in a game show where I would be the host and they would be the contestants. I told them to put their hands on imaginary buzzers and then I would ask a trivia question almost anyone could answer such as, "What is the name of Mickey Mouse's girlfriend?" Whoever buzzed in first and correctly answered the question won a dollar. I'd usually give away five dollars a day this way. Not only was this the perfect way for me to synthesize my interest in game shows but I also got people to interact with me in a situation where I was in control.

One day a classmate who I came to respect a lot approached me and said, "Look, Nick. I feel bad about taking money from you." He gave me back the money he'd just won.

I was puzzled. "You're not taking it from me. You earned it by answering the question right."

A few days later, my homeroom teacher pulled me aside and told me that kids were taking advantage of me. "No, they're not," I said. "I asked them to play the game and they agreed. They're earning the money, fair and square."

At the time, I actually believed this to be true. Now of course I can understand how desperate I was to connect with others. My naivety, a common Asperger's trait, was blinding me to the message that "money can't buy me love," so clearly expressed in The Beatles song. Many years later, after I was diagnosed with Asperger's, I was able to put my behavior in this situation into context and it made much more sense to me.

Throughout the years my dad had been trying to interest me in various sports but the only one I was good at, or even liked, was tennis. In elementary school I started taking lessons at a local club. Even though I was short and rather clumsy, I developed solid strokes and a decent serve. By seventh grade I had turned into a serious player and started to play in tournaments. In my first six matches I suffered six straight lopsided defeats. Even though I was losing consistently, my dad encouraged me to keep trying. "You're getting better with each match, Nick," he'd tell me. "Just stick with it and you'll end up victorious one of these days." He was right.

One day I was playing a consolation match against a boy named Cory and everything seemed to click. I won in straight sets. Afterwards Cory asked me for my phone number in case I ever wanted to hit balls with him in the future. It was the first time anyone had ever initiated a social encounter with me outside of my parents setting up play dates for me when I was much younger. Suddenly, a light bulb went on in my head: so this is the way you make friends. You win tennis matches. You show others how good you are at something. From that day on, I felt motivated and started to win more and more matches.

Becoming a good tennis player became the most important goal in my life. I devoted myself full time to the sport and also began videotaping and studying professional tennis matches. I'd watch certain points from those games over and over again and became enthralled by the geometric angles and precise accuracy of players like John McEnroe, Ivan Lendl, and Andre Agassi. By the end of middle school, I had won a number of local tournaments and was being recognized in the tennis community as a player to be reckoned with. It was a miracle. Here I was, this chunky, little kid who was not very athletic, but had somehow managed to become a tennis champion. It was a little like Forrest Gump winning the All American Award for college football. Who could have predicted it?

Unfortunately, no other students at my middle school played tennis with any degree of seriousness, so I would either meet other kids interested in tennis at the local club where I took lessons or at various tournaments. Eventually, I made a few tennis friends outside of school and regularly got together with them to hit balls or play games. Finally, I was connecting with other kids and could engage in a special interest that I really enjoyed. That felt good.

In the summer of seventh grade, I attended a tennis camp for a week with Jake, a tennis friend, and his friend, Spencer. The camp was at Oberlin College and the three of us shared a dormitory room. One day, Jake and Spencer started calling me Rain Man in reference to the autistic character Dustin Hoffman played in the movie of the same name. In retrospect, I believe this reference was prompted because I was constantly spouting off tennis statistics in an attempt to impress Jake and Spencer with my vast knowledge of tennis. But at the time I was very hurt and angry with them for calling me that name. Rain Man was autistic. I certainly wasn't autistic. Why in the world would Jake and Spencer compare me to someone like that? Only time would solve that riddle.

I had my Bar Mitzvah at fourteen instead of the traditional age of thirteen because I was a year behind my classmates both at temple and at school. It was both a joyous and a lonely experience. The joyous part was the speech I delivered to the congregation on the day of my Bar Mitzvah. It was customary at our temple for the Bar Mitzvah boy to select an exemplary Jewish hero, research this person, and then give a presentation to family, friends, and the congregation. For my hero, I chose George Burns, the famous entertainer, because of his great sense of humor and zest for life. Giving my presentation to over a hundred people was one of the high points of my life. It was the first time I ever got up in front of a group to speak and it felt very positive and empowering. The audience laughed in all the right places and they were clearly laughing with me, not at me. Afterwards, I received lavish praise from both the rabbi and the congregation about what a good speaker I was. I felt a surge of confidence from the whole experience.

The lonely part of my Bar Mitzvah was the party that was held the next day. It is typical for the Bar Mitzvah boy to have a party where he invites all his friends. Fortunately, I had recently made the transition at school from social outcast to geeky eccentric. Shooting three pointers, doing the preacher routine, and giving away money had all helped. I was still being bullied but most kids were starting to see that I was too nice a guy to beat down and they started to back off a little. Because of this upgrade in my social status, I felt enough confidence to invite some classmates to my Bar Mitzvah party.

The truth of the situation was that none of these classmates were my friends although most of them accepted my invitation, I believe in part, because they wanted to attend a Whirlyball party, a social activity that combines bumper cars and lacrosse in a specially built arena. Even though it was over twenty years ago, I can recall how I felt that day. It was as if I was attending someone else's party, not my own. No one came up to talk to me, which was strange because normally the Bar Mitzvah boy is the center of attention. I could feel myself detaching mentally and not wanting to be at my own party. I intuitively sensed that none of the kids were actually there to celebrate with me. Instead, they just wanted to play Whirlyball on a Sunday afternoon. Lesley Gore's hit song, "It's My Party and I'll Cry if I Want To," perfectly describes my emotional experience that day. Only twenty-four hours earlier, I had been in my glory after giving my speech. Now I felt lonely at my own party. It was a sad reminder of how isolated I still was from my peers.

Ironically, one of the saddest days of middle school was graduation. I should have been happy to get out of that horrible hellhole, but at the party where everyone was happily reminiscing about the past three years, I was sitting all alone with a cup of fruit punch in my hand. I realized that in all three years of middle school I had not made a single friend.

The next day, the entire eighth grade class took a graduation trip to Cedar Point, one of the biggest amusement parks in the United States. As I walked by the roller coaster, the Ferris wheel, and the hotdog stand, I felt no sense of celebration. Wandering around the park by myself I saw two of my classmates, a boy and girl, kissing. I suddenly realized just how emotionally behind I really was. Kissing a girl was something I should be interested in doing at this age but I wasn't. It was further proof of what a failure I perceived myself to be. Unlike everyone else who was enjoying themselves at Cedar Point, I couldn't wait to get back on that bus and return to the safety of my home.

High school was just around the corner and I was aware that I could finally stand out in a meaningful way for something I could do well. There had been no tennis team in middle school but there was one in high school. On the bus ride back to Detroit from Cedar Point, I thought about how playing tennis in high school might give me the chance to redeem myself after three miserable years in middle school.

CHAPTER 4
High School
Wins and Losses

As a freshman entering high school, I couldn't wait to try out for the varsity tennis team. Tennis was going to be my saving grace and my goal was to play number one singles. I had no idea how tryouts would go, but I knew that my main rival in local tournaments was also trying out for the team.

Jeffrey and I had been playing opposite each other for several years. He was a highly ranked player who was also rather cocky. I had beaten him in the finals of a few tournaments and I could tell he was embarrassed whenever he lost to me. At one tournament, right in the middle of a match where I was ahead, he retired early claiming he didn't feel well. His father later told my dad that he was angry with Jeffrey for feigning illness rather than losing to me again. I guess it was demoralizing for a jock like Jeffrey to be defeated by someone who often wore mismatched socks and Velcro tennis shoes and sometimes cried if he lost a tough match.

Though we were only high school freshmen, the number one singles slot on the varsity team eventually came down to Jeffrey and me. We both desperately wanted the position but for different reasons. Jeffrey did not want to be playing below someone he viewed as a pathetic misfit, and I wanted to prove to my peers that I was the best at something. In order to decide who would get the top slot, the coach had us play a few challenge matches. Every time Jeffrey lost, he was unwilling to concede and would insist on a rematch. After several of these matches, the coach had seen enough and decided that I would be the number one singles player.

In an effort to undermine my accomplishment, Jeffrey decided to play a practical joke on me. One day the team was playing an away match on the east side of Detroit. As the last game was ending, the coach asked me to go around the block and tell the bus driver that we were almost ready to leave. When I came back, I saw that Jeffrey was in tears. I asked him what was wrong and he told me he had just lost a close match. I tried to console him, but he just kept crying. It was strange. Jeffrey was a sore loser but I had never seen him act this way.

When we got on the bus, I noticed my teammates were snickering and laughing under their breath. I didn't understand why they would find this situation funny. After a few more snickers, Jeffrey finally said, "Hey Nick. I didn't lose the match. I was just imitating you when you lose a match." Everyone then broke into hysterics including the coach. I couldn't believe it. They had all put on an act just to embarrass me. The actions of Jeffrey and my teammates hurt my feelings, but I was devastated that my coach would go along with their prank. Later, when I told my dad what had happened, he was very angry with the coach and gave him an earful. To his credit, the coach apologized to me and acknowledged how inappropriately he behaved. In retrospect, I think I understand why the coach behaved so immaturely. This was his first coaching job and he was only a few years older than the players. Also, he was trying to win over a team that would much rather have had Jeffrey as the number one singles player.

Besides dealing with Jeffrey's antagonism, I realized that being number one on the tennis team didn't necessarily make me popular with the other players. The main reason I wanted to play number one was to be liked by my teammates. That didn't happen. Although they respected and admired my tennis skills, they never included me socially when they did things outside of school. I wasn't invited to parties or just to hang out with any of them. The truth was I had virtually nothing in common with my teammates other than tennis. It was like being the star quarterback of a high school football team but the least popular member of the team. I had expected my athletic talent to lead to popularity and acceptance, but that was not the case. Without knowing I had Asperger's at the time, there was nothing to explain why I was so socially isolated from the rest of the team.

Being socially isolated was not only confined to the tennis team. In the summer of ninth grade, I participated in the Maccabi Games, a Jewish Junior Olympics-style sports competition that is held in a different city each year. I traveled to St Louis as a member of the Detroit tennis team. Part of the Maccabi tradition is that participants stay with host families who offer to sponsor two athletes for the week. Thousands of athletes from all over the world converge to spend a week competing in their sport as well as socializing with their fellow athletes at a number of social events. I avoided going to most of these events and once even faked being sick to get out of attending a party. Other than my interactions with the adults who were hosting me, I didn't connect with anyone the whole week I was there.

In addition to my social isolation, I also felt emotionally and sexually much younger than my peers. Although I was playing number one singles on my varsity tennis team, most of the time I felt like a ten-year-old. For example, I came home from school every day to eat lunch and watch television by myself rather than staying on campus. This behavior was certainly atypical and my mom was very concerned about it. She encouraged me to stay at school the whole day but I simply couldn't tolerate being there for seven hours without a break.

My special interests also reflected my immaturity. I still preferred to watch the 1980 Wimbledon men's finals on videotape for the eighty-fifth time rather than a live broadcast of the Super Bowl. Game shows and tennis statistics still took up most of my free time. Special interests rarely have anything to do with popular culture. I didn't understand why other kids liked Madonna, *Beavis and Butt-head*, or *The Simpsons*. On New Year's Eve in ninth grade, I chose to attend an Al Green concert with my parents rather than go to a party with kids my age. I knew this preference wasn't normal but I liked spending time with my mom and dad. Most teenagers rebel against their parents and want to be with their friends all the time, but as an adolescent I clung even tighter to my parents as if they were a security blanket that brought me comfort. As I had told my guidance counselor during the first few weeks of middle school, I always wished I could turn back the clock.

Some of the best times I had in high school were spent alone with my dad when he and I would travel to out-of-state tennis tournaments. These tournaments were United States Tennis Association sanctioned and were not related to the high school season. On these road trips, I had my dad all to myself. It reminded me of the time I used to spend with him as a little boy. I could be totally myself around my dad. If I lost a match, I could have a meltdown in front of him and not feel ashamed. If I was nervous before a match, I could share my fears and insecurities with him and he would always help me to relax. He would sit there and calmly reassure me that no matter what happened everything was going to be all right.

Apart from not connecting socially with my high school teammates, there were certain unexplained sexual feelings I was having towards some of them. These feelings made no sense to me but created great discomfort and, occasionally, even thoughts of suicide. In the mid 1990s when I was in high school, there was very little enlightenment on the subject of gay, lesbian, and transgender issues. I often heard the word "fag" being casually tossed around in the hallways, the locker room, and even on the tennis court. Being thought of as gay was about the lowest opinion anyone could have of you.

In spite of my sexual confusion, I still assumed I was straight and that these attractions were just a phase I was going through. I didn't understand what was going on with my sexuality, which explains why I was so sexually confused. I still hoped I would catch up soon and start socializing at age-appropriate levels with the guys on the tennis team. If that were possible, then perhaps I would start being interested in girls. I desperately hoped my heterosexual desires were just delayed and waiting for the right opportunity to emerge. After all, if someone has never gone skiing in his life, how can he know for certain that he doesn't like to ski? Since I hadn't experienced what all the other guys had, maybe I simply didn't know what I was missing.

In 1994 when I was in tenth grade, my parents discovered a summer tennis program called Tennis Europe that offered advanced teen tennis players the chance to travel to different cities in Europe to compete in various tournaments over a three-week period. Because of my experiences with the Maccabi Games and at the Oberlin tennis camp, I initially resisted the idea. Being away from home was never easy for me, but being separated from my parents for three whole weeks while being on a different continent seemed far too overwhelming. My parents worried about my overdependence on them and my lack of socializing. From their perspective, Tennis Europe could address both these issues. My dad started to work on me. He repeatedly asked when I would get this kind of opportunity again. When would I be able to go to the top of the Eiffel Tower and overlook one of the most beautiful cities in the world? When would I have the chance to go to a Belgian chocolate factory and taste the finest chocolate in the world? He was very persuasive. He reminded me that I loved playing competitive tennis and that it would also be a nice break from my high school teammates. I was sold.

My dad and I drove from Detroit to JFK airport in New York City where I was to meet my Tennis Europe teammates. On the Pennsylvania turnpike, I remember a sudden feeling of terror gripping me. I now know it was an acute anxiety attack. I started sweating profusely and my whole body felt paralyzed. I remember telling my dad that I felt as if I was going to lose my freedom for the next three weeks. Baffled, he looked at me and said, "Nick, it's just the opposite. What you're about to experience is total freedom." What my dad didn't understand was that, for me, spending three weeks in close proximity with a group of teenagers I didn't know and who I was sure wouldn't like me was not my idea of freedom. It felt more like a punishment. I was scared to death, but it was too late to back out now.

Saying goodbye to my dad at JFK was the most frightening moment of my life so far. Suddenly, he was gone and I was left standing there with eight teenagers and two adult chaperones, all strangers to me. *Damn it, Dad. Why did you have to leave me here?* I thought. *I'm not ready for this! I can't be away from you for this long!* But I had to face reality. My dad was on his way back to Detroit and I was off to Paris, France on a Boeing 747 to spend three long weeks traveling through Europe.

I got off to a slow start. On the long overseas flight I sat alone and didn't talk to anyone until I was introduced to my roommate in Paris. Jason immediately struck me as a good guy. He was a cultured teen from Rye, New York and unlike anyone I had ever met before. As a matter of fact, most of my Tennis Europe teammates were much different from the kids I knew back home. These were sophisticated East Coast teenagers who were more liberal and much friendlier than my classmates in suburban Detroit. I particularly liked Jason. He played a number of instruments, knew a lot about all kinds of music, and could converse on a high level about Frank Sinatra with me. He saw that I kept listening over and over to the same Sinatra tape on my Walkman and asked if I ever listened to anything besides Sinatra. "Man, there's so much more out there," he said. Jason introduced me to artists I had never heard of before, like Nina Simone and other female jazz divas. I immediately fell in love with their music. Why didn't more kids like Jason exist back home?

Jason and I talked about our lives at home. He was popular, had many girlfriends, and played in a hard rock band that had gigs at various clubs on the upper east side of Manhattan. My roommate was a rock star and he was still in high school. How cool! He smoked pot and even boasted of going all the way on a few occasions with his girlfriend. How could I compete with that? I couldn't. So I lied. I told Jason I too had a girlfriend, that I had had several previous girlfriends, and that I also had gone all the way. I felt really horrible telling those lies to Jason. How could I stoop so low? Perhaps Jason knew that I was lying but was sensitive enough not to burst my bubble. Jason was the type of person who liked to befriend outsiders. He told me that some of his friends at school were social outcasts who were often bullied and it made him feel good to spend time with those kids. I wondered why he was telling me this. Did it apply to me, too? I never told Jason that I too was bullied because I didn't want him to see me in a different light.

Jason almost seemed like a big brother after a while because he was so much more mature than me. We were both the same age but it sure didn't feel that way. I had the emotional maturity of a pre-adolescent while he seemed wise, experienced, and older than his seventeen years. I also began to have emotional and physical feelings for Jason that, at the time, I didn't understand. These feelings were extremely confusing and uncomfortable for me. I was really scared. The way I felt seemed wrong, dirty, and even sinful. I hated myself and yet I couldn't help how I felt. I became extremely guarded because I didn't want these feelings to become apparent to Jason.

One of the most memorable times of the trip took place in Antwerp, Belgium. I was playing in a tournament against one of the top twelve-year-old tennis players in all of Belgium. I was five years older than he was, but based on his skills, it didn't feel that way. Normally, my opponents were my age or older. I always felt five years younger than them in terms of emotional maturity even though I could beat most of them.

My young Belgian opponent defeated me in the first set, winning every game. There was a large group of supporters cheering him on while my Tennis Europe teammates were rooting for me. As he took a commanding lead in the second set, the cheering from his camp became louder and louder. This lit a fuse under me. On the brink of defeat I suddenly thought, *I can't let this twelve-year-old defeat me in front of my teammates.* Normally, if I were about to lose a match, I would feel sad and resigned about the impending defeat but not this time.

I refused to be humiliated by an opponent who was the same age as the kids who bullied me in middle school. I decided I wasn't going to take it any longer. From that moment on, I shifted gears. After a three-hour battle that emotionally and physically wore me out, I won the match. Despite the age difference, my opponent was the odds on favorite, but my determination rose to a level I had never experienced before. I felt possessed and yet it seemed to have nothing to do with tennis. I felt that losing this match to a twelve-year-old in front of my Tennis Europe teammates was simply not an option. I eventually went on to win the entire tournament in Antwerp, Belgium.

Another memorable part of the trip was being allowed to roam around the city of Amsterdam alone. Jason was hanging out with another group of guys and I figured I would enjoy some solitary exploration. At some point, I found myself in the Red Light District. This area was quite an eye-opening experience for me since I had no sexual experience. I couldn't believe how open sexuality was in Amsterdam as compared with the way I perceived it back home.

During my three weeks in Europe, I called my parents at least once a day. I desperately missed them and couldn't believe how long it would be until I saw them again. This separation gave me a glimpse of what it might feel like when both of them died and I would be on my own. As long as I can recall, the fear of my parents dying has always been with me. That's why I called them every day from Europe just to make sure that they were still safe and sound. Because this was in 1994 and cellphones weren't commercially available yet, it was quite a chore to find a pay phone every day. Sometimes I'd be lucky enough to be able to call them from my hotel room when Jason wasn't there, but if on a particular day I wasn't able to reach them, I would totally panic.

After Tennis Europe ended, I was thrilled to see my parents back in New York where they picked me up at JFK. The first thing I did after getting off the plane was to confess to them that I had lied to my teammates during the trip. I admitted I had made up an entire social life that didn't exist. It was embarrassing to share this with my parents, but that's how guilty I felt and how much I needed to get it off my chest. Overall, Tennis Europe had been a good experience for me. Early in the trip, it was clear that I was the best player on the team, and in this setting as opposed to high school, being a good player not only brought me respect but also the social acceptance I had been yearning for and never had received.

When I returned home, I didn't think I would ever see any of my Tennis Europe teammates again, but Jason and another teammate, Sam, invited me to meet them in New York the following fall to attend the men's final of the US Open in New York. It was a thrill watching my hero, Andre Agassi, win his first US Open championship against Michael Stitch and spending a few days with two of my friends from Tennis Europe.

After the visit to New York, I could never bring myself to call Jason or Sam. I never heard from Jason but occasionally Sam would call me. I was always glad to talk to him but I would never initiate a call to him. Why didn't I try to maintain these friendships? In retrospect, I don't think I was comfortable dealing with the confusing feelings I had towards Jason. With Sam, I was just scared of being rejected like I had been so many other times in my life. Eventually Sam stopped calling. My mom was upset about my unwillingness to keep these friendships going. She was constantly after me to give these guys a call. She thought I was blowing an opportunity to have friends and she told me so in no uncertain terms. Truth be told, she was right.

The following summer in 1995, I began my first job teaching tennis at a wealthy suburban country club. My boss had heard of me because he knew I was a highly ranked player and asked me if I would work full time as a tennis instructor over the summer. Since my dad was encouraging me to find a job, this opportunity seemed much better than working at some type of minimum wage employment.

Soon after I started the job, my boss, Aaron, started to notice my eccentricities. As always, I was having trouble making small talk with staff and club members. I never got their jokes, and my disinterest in what they talked about was evident to them, I'm sure. Also, my poor fine motor skills made it difficult to do certain simple tasks, like painting straight lines on the tennis court. Aaron not only poked fun at me but he often did so in front of the kids who were there to take lessons. He would refer to me as "the waddler," because he thought I walked like a penguin, a nickname I didn't appreciate. He would also call me "pork-barrel boy" because I was a little overweight. One day, he really crossed the line. When I went to use the bathroom in the clubhouse, he encouraged several kids to hold the door shut so I couldn't get out. At first I thought I had locked myself in, so I kept pushing and pushing, but the force on the other end was too great. Then I heard laughter coming from Aaron and the kids and realized they were all playing a prank on me. History was again repeating itself. It was just like being handcuffed to the swing in fifth grade and being pranked by my high school team and the coach. Here I was eighteen years old and a tennis pro at a prestigious country club, but I was still being bullied and humiliated by both children and adults. Finally I heard Aaron say, "Okay, he's had enough. Let him out." I ran out of the bathroom in tears and headed straight for my car. That was my last day on the job. I refused to be victimized by bullies any more, regardless of their age.

During my senior year of high school, I became an All-State tennis player, which was publicized in several newspapers. I also won Regionals, was named Most Valuable Player on my high school team and was ranked the number one player in Southeastern Michigan for my age group. These athletic accomplishments were juxtaposed against my mediocre academic performance. While I was busy trying to prove myself as a tennis player, I completely neglected my academic studies. Similar to my pattern in middle school, I had no energy to devote to schoolwork that seemed inconsequential to me. I had more important things to be concerned about. Namely, I wanted recognition and I knew making the honor roll wasn't on the cards for me. Most of my classes like algebra, biology, literature, and world history were subjects I wasn't interested in or had no aptitude for. Since a lot of my class work was so difficult, I simply neglected it and sought recognition in other ways.

Given my longstanding interest in game shows and their hosts, broadcasting was the one class I really wanted to take. I liked projecting a certain kind of voice, not unlike some game show hosts, and thought I could mimic them doing the daily announcements over the loudspeaker. I was excited to sign up for the class, but the broadcasting teacher, Mrs Bowen, had concerns that my fine motor difficulties would make it hard for me to set up the reel-to-reel tape machine that was used every day. She thought that if I needed assistance every time the machine needed to be set up, I would slow everyone else down in preparing for the daily broadcast. Mrs Bowen came to one of my Individualized Education Plan meetings specifically to tell my parents, my special education teacher, and me that it would not be in my best interest to take the class.

Shocked and angry, my parents turned to the special education teacher to help advocate for me, but to their surprise and dismay, she agreed with Mrs Bowen. My parents and I sat there stunned. Hearing both the special education teacher and the broadcasting teacher veto my taking the class made me doubt whether I even wanted to take it. If these two teachers agreed, maybe they knew what they were talking about. But my mom was outraged and spoke her mind. She felt there could be an accommodation, like having someone help me on the days I had to do the reel-to-reel set up, that would make the situation workable. She said that to deny me the opportunity to excel at something in which I was interested, based solely on my fine motor problems was blatantly unfair and discriminatory. My parents refused to back down. They wanted me to feel good about myself in an area other than tennis and insisted that I be given the chance to take the class. After a week of thinking about it, Mrs Bowen finally relented and said I would be allowed to take the class but only on a trial basis. The accommodation was put in place. I did need assistance when it was my turn to set up the reel-to-reel, but it wasn't the big deal Mrs Bowen had thought it would be.

I loved doing the daily announcements over the loudspeaker; they were broadcast throughout the entire school. I had a trademark way of starting them, as if I were the Robin Williams character in the movie, *Good Morning, Vietnam*. "Gooooood morning, Seaholm High!" I would say. If this wasn't a good way to get everyone's attention, I didn't know what was. This salutation certainly got me noticed around school.

Besides broadcasting, another class I found interesting was social psychology. I liked learning about what made people behave the way they did. However, one day the teacher had the class do an exercise that proved to be very uncomfortable for me. She had us take out a separate piece of paper for every student in the class, write their name on it, and then list three adjectives that best described that individual. This was all done anonymously. The teacher then collected all of the sheets of paper and passed the specific comments to the person who was being described. As I read the various adjectives my classmates had written about me, I consistently came across these words: really weird, strange, different, paces around the room, and kind of funny but clueless. If I had needed further proof that I was perceived as different from my peers, I now had it.

Graduation from high school, just like middle school, was a sad experience for me. My parents wanted to throw a graduation party for me; I was adamant that I did not want one because I knew I wasn't going to feel celebratory about this occasion and the thought of being at the center of a social event was totally unappealing. My parents were equally adamant that my graduation needed to be celebrated and a huge fight ensued between us.

One area of contention between us was that I didn't want to have a party on the same day as the graduation ceremony. It was too much stimulation for me. Perhaps if I had been aware of having Asperger's at the time, I could have expressed my feelings in a way that my parents would have understood, but my mom and dad prevailed and had a brunch at our house following the ceremony, mostly attended by their friends and relatives. The photographs that were taken that day clearly show how unhappy I was. I look like I just came from, or was on my way to, a funeral. Reflecting back on that time, I can now see that my parents just wanted to be like a normal family and celebrate an event that most people view as a happy occasion.

Besides the party my parents were giving, there was also an official high school graduation party at the local community center. The party was held on the same day as the graduation ceremony and was scheduled to last all night. This was far too much social activity for me—the graduation ceremony, the brunch at my parents' house and an all-night party with my classmates—all within twenty-four hours. I refused to attend the school-sponsored party because I knew it would be another agonizing night spent alone in a crowd, but my parents put a lot of pressure on me to go and so I finally did.

I arrived around 8:00 p.m. and soon learned that the adult organizers of the event weren't letting students leave the premises until the next morning to prevent them from going off somewhere and drinking. This restriction frustrated me as I was planning to leave the party after twenty minutes or so. As I walked around the carnival-like atmosphere of the party, I felt almost identical to the way I had four years ago on the Cedar Point middle school graduation trip.

Every minute of the party, I was preoccupied with wanting to go home. I didn't want to spend one more minute at this dreadful event than was absolutely necessary. My classmates were all very sad about leaving their friends behind to go off to college. Friends? What friends? I felt like Scrooge. Bah Humbug. Screw high school! By 11:00 p.m. I'd had enough and mustered up the courage to approach one of the adult organizers of the event and asked her to call my parents so I could get permission to leave. I told her I was not feeling well, which was psychologically true. Fortunately, my parents answered the phone and did not seem surprised to get my phone call. They gave their consent and I left the party, finally closing the chapter on my life in the public schools once and for all.

So, after four years of high school, what were the wins and losses? I played number one singles and was captain of my tennis team, and yet I didn't make a single friend. I was recognized for my unique way of doing the morning announcements, but I was still sexually confused and alienated from my classmates. And although I had traveled across Europe and had been separated from my parents for three weeks, I still felt joined at the hip to them.

At least I had managed to graduate with a grade point average of 3.0, quite an achievement given my lack of effort. Fortunately, standards for getting into a decent college were not as high then as they are today. To my surprise, I was accepted into a well-regarded state university on the western side of Michigan that had a very good tennis team and excellent support services for special education students. After meeting with the tennis coach and touring the campus, I decided to attend Grand Valley State University in the fall. Even though I had always had great difficulty being away from home, I never considered going to a local university. Everyone else was going away to college and so would I. The biggest worry that I had was whether I could survive being on my own one hundred and seventy miles away from my parents for an entire year.

CHAPTER 5

Freshman Year of College

The Brink of Despair

As I reflect on my nineteen-year-old self when I first entered college in 1996, it is hard to believe that I was actually considered a legal adult. I felt like a much younger person who made a very adult decision to leave home and attend a university one hundred and seventy miles away. At the time, I thought I had valid reasons for making this decision: Grand Valley State had a good academic reputation, a tennis team where I had a chance to play number one singles, and excellent support services for special education students.

What influenced my decision the most was that almost everyone I graduated from high school with was going away to college. I wanted to be like everyone else and not be judged as a loser who stayed home with Mommy and Daddy and went to a local college. Looking back, I'm surprised that my decision was never up for debate in my mind. The strong belief that I should go away to college completely blocked out my real emotional needs at that time. Only three months earlier during my senior year of high school, I was still going home for lunch every day and had virtually no social life. It seemed that my parents interpreted my decision to leave home and venture out of the nest as a sign of maturity and growth. Whereas I had always resisted any kind of separation from my parents in the past, I now appeared to embrace it.

It was important for me to have my own car at college so I could drive home on weekends. Therefore, the day my parents dropped me off at Grand Valley State, we caravanned to the campus in separate cars. The further we got from home, the more scared I became. As I looked back at my parents through the rear view mirror, I began to sob uncontrollably. *What have I gotten myself into?* I thought. *How can I handle this experience when I've done nothing to prepare for it? How can I be away from my parents for weeks or months at a time?*

The truth is, from the moment I made the decision to go to Grand Valley, I had serious doubts about whether I could survive being away from home. But I vehemently fought against those fears. I engaged in major self-deception in an effort to convince myself that any nineteen-year-old, including me, should be able to leave home by that age. This rationalization trumped all my past experience, which clearly told me I was not ready to make the leap into independent living.

My parents and I arrived at Grand Valley on a late August afternoon. Almost immediately, I was introduced to my roommate. I sensed that we had nothing in common except for the fact that we were both Grand Valley students. He was from a small town in Michigan and had nothing to say to me. I tried being friendly but it was obvious from the start that we weren't going to be compatible. After my parents witnessed this awkward introduction, I begged them not to leave. But all three of us knew that was impossible. It was time for them to go. My parents and I tearfully hugged each other goodbye and then they departed for Detroit. My mother told me she cried all the way home.

The first three weeks of college were a living hell for me. I had always spent a great deal of time alone, but now there were people around me constantly and I didn't like it one bit. On top of that I had to share a room the size of a large closet with another human being. I was used to peace and quiet, but dorm life was noisy and chaotic. Loud, heavy metal music was blasting out of most of the dorm rooms at all hours of the day and night. It was a sensory nightmare for someone with Asperger's who was very sensitive to sound.

In order to reduce my discomfort, I bought my first white noise machine to block out the dorm racket so that I could sleep. I asked my roommate if he objected to the noise machine and with a complete look of disdain, he told me he didn't. As it turned out, the use of the machine had no effect on him. Most of the time, he came and went at all hours of the night while I tried in vain to get some sleep. In spite of the noise machine, my roommate was interrupting my sleep every night with his constant comings and goings. When I asked him if he could be quieter when opening and shutting the door, his response was to ignore me.

After the first week of school, I couldn't wait to get away from my roommate as well as Grand Valley so I made the one hundred and seventy mile drive back home. On my way home, I stopped at a music store near downtown Grand Rapids and bought a Count Basie CD. For the next fifteen weekends, with only one exception, I drove home every Friday and started the trip by playing that Basie CD as soon as I left school. Basie's joyously spirited music took on a profound symbolic significance for me. The songs served as a musical backdrop for the drive home, representing what I called the hymns of freedom because as I was listening to this music I felt liberated; I was returning to a life of familiarity and security.

Most college freshmen take pride in living away from home and acquiring their independence, but for me it was just the opposite. I only felt free to be myself when I was safe and secure at home with my parents. The chaos and confusion that surrounded me at college made me feel as if I was in prison. Every weekend was an emotionally draining experience. On Fridays, I would drive home on a euphoric high and by Sunday I would return to Grand Valley completely depressed. If anyone asked me how I survived that year traveling three hundred and forty miles round trip every weekend, I would have to say Count Basie helped me get through it.

Every weekend I was at home, I would watch old home videos of myself from elementary school, reveling in that time period and wishing I could turn back the clock and be that age again. As I watched those home movies, I felt an emotional identification with my elementary school-aged self and an emotional disconnect with my current-aged self. These home movies fed my need for the nostalgia of simpler times in my life, which helped rejuvenate me in the short time I spent at home. Leaving home each Sunday was always an emotional upheaval for me. I would cry and my parents would be distraught, but there was nothing to be done but go back and live through another week.

During the week at Grand Valley, I would call home at least several times a day. These were not brief calls to touch base with my parents. They were often hour-long conversations, especially with my dad, where I would talk about how lonely I was and how I didn't know how I would get through another day, let alone a whole year. My dad tried his best to tell me that things would get better, but his encouragement fell on deaf ears.

One particular weekday evening the power went out in the dorm because of a severe thunderstorm. This was a serious emergency for me because I knew I wouldn't be able to use my noise machine since it could only be plugged in and didn't operate on batteries. This power outage seemed to spark an even rowdier atmosphere in the dorm than usual. As a result of this sudden and unexpected occurrence, I had a gigantic meltdown. Panic stricken and out-of-control, I frantically went searching for my residential advisor (RA) in the darkened corridors of the dorm. I was stomping my feet and crying and my voice was raised to the point of yelling. I'm surprised my RA didn't try to have me committed to a mental institution.

I told her that I couldn't cope with what was happening. She nodded and listened patiently but I'm sure she didn't understand my desperate emotional state. I asked her for permission to go somewhere else for the night. She laughed and said that she wasn't my mother and that I didn't need her permission to leave the dorm. So I went to a nearby hotel and checked in for the night. Then, I called my mom in a very disturbed state and told her what had happened. My mom was genuinely puzzled that I had checked into a hotel. Why couldn't I just stay on campus? What was the big deal? Mom's reaction pissed me off. Didn't she remember that I was the same person who used to come home every day for lunch only a few months ago? If my own mother couldn't understand why I was so overwhelmed, then who could? Of course, today I don't blame my mom for having that reaction. She didn't have the whole story regarding my Asperger's and, of course, neither did I.

By the end of the third week of classes, dorm life had become absolutely intolerable for me and I was ready to drop out of school. Instead of driving home that weekend, I met my parents at a resort outside of South Haven, Michigan, where we had often gone on summer vacations. I think my parents felt that meeting there might bring a sense of happier times and lift my spirits. I wanted to talk to my dad alone so the two of us took a ride in the country. I told him that if I had to spend one more week in the dorm, I would either drop out of school or commit suicide. He could tell that I meant it. This was the first time I had ever mentioned any kind of suicidal ideation and my father took me seriously. He vowed to come up with a workable solution to this dilemma. He also told me that if I could find the courage to hang on and finish the year, he would take me to Los Angeles to see a live taping of *The Price Is Right* with host Bob Barker, my all-time favorite television show since I was a toddler. This strategy was pure genius and the promise he made to take me to *The Price Is Right* went a long way towards motivating me to finish the school year.

The week after we met in South Haven, my dad called and said that he had found a rooming house about three miles away from the Grand Valley campus. The couple who lived there had an extra bedroom in the basement that they rented out. I could live there and drive to campus every day. The house was way out in the boonies in a totally rural environment.

Without any hesitation, I decided to move out of the dorm and into the rooming house. It wasn't the perfect situation, but leaving the dorm temporarily helped buoy my spirits. Being in a house of any kind, even one that was isolated and next to a cornfield, felt more comfortable to me than living in the dorm. It was quiet and I didn't have to be surrounded by drunk and disorderly college students.

Although the boarding house was peaceful, I wasn't really comfortable hanging out in someone else's house. I also had no interest in being on campus or socializing with other students, so almost every day after I was done with my classes and studying, I passed the time taking long drives around the suburbs of Grand Rapids, which was twenty-five miles from campus. These daily rides probably only make sense if one understands Asperger's. I was used to living in the suburbs and had never lived in a rural area before. In retrospect, I was trying to recreate the physical surroundings of my parents' neighborhood and what was familiar to me. I'd look for lush tree-lined streets with two-story colonial homes and sidewalks because these neighborhoods made me feel as if I were home again. Even if this wasn't actually the case, I always had Fridays to look forward to where I could enjoy the real thing.

I also spent much of the time on those drives at all-you-can-eat food buffets. I didn't realize it at the time but I was sublimating all my anxiety and depression into food. That year, I developed a binge eating disorder and started consuming enormous quantities of food. My weeks were ritualized in such a way that I'd eat at a different buffet each day of the week. Following these routines was of paramount importance to me. I put on about fifteen pounds by the end of the first semester, which was scary because the tennis season was fast approaching.

During my first semester, I took a philosophy class that had a critical impact on me. While the class brought something very positive and new into my life, it also created an existential crisis. On the positive side, the content of the course opened my mind to various philosophical ideas and questions that I had never considered before. Being introduced to the philosophies of great thinkers like Plato, Hegel, Schopenhauer, Nietzsche, and even Freud, felt like meeting very special friends for the first time. Their collective ideas stimulated new avenues of intellectual discovery. I attribute the reawakening of my intellectual curiosity, which had been dormant since middle school, to this philosophy course.

This course also took a costly emotional toll on me. My professor, who frequently referenced the Christian reformer, John Calvin, was openly prejudiced against homosexuals. During his last lecture before final exams, this professor specifically referred to homosexuality as a defect and said that homosexuals were morally bankrupt individuals. He even compared homosexuality to bestiality. He also painted a picture of the renowned twentieth-century sex researcher and pioneer, Alfred Kinsey, as one of the most fraudulent men in the history of science. He made Kinsey sound like nothing more than an opportunist. Since then, I've read a lot about Dr Kinsey and have come to regard him as a brave champion of sexual equality for gays, lesbians, and transgendered individuals as well as a proponent of women's rights.

Because I was so suggestible, I believed this professor, with his divinity and philosophy degrees from Calvin College and Harvard University, must be right about homosexuality. The strong words he used in his lecture created intense discomfort in me. I had been having same-sex attractions for some time. Maybe I was this defective, disgusting excuse for a human being that he had described. For the past several years, I had been terrified that someone I knew, including my own parents, would discover my sexual confusion. My professor's comments had the effect of stirring the pot, bringing those fears to a boil and then magnifying them in my mind way out of proportion. I began to really believe that I was gay. I started to feel paranoid and even suicidal. I had been called gay many times in middle school and even in a couple of instances in high school, but none of those people actually knew whether I was gay. What if it was true? Would I be the victim of a hate crime? Would someone even try to kill me if this information got out? Would my parents disown me? I probably didn't even deserve to live. I was a terrible person.

Having these feelings about my sexual orientation was very painful, but as strange as this may sound, I was also having difficulty coming to terms with the fact that I was a sexual being at all. I wasn't just worried about being gay, although that disgusted me to even think about. What I wanted was to be asexual. In other words, I wanted to deny myself any and all sexual impulses because they felt so confusing to me. Socially, my life was challenging enough that I didn't want to add an even more complicated element to it—namely, sex.

However, I couldn't deny I was a sexual being who had fantasies and attractions. I was living in an adult body. It was obvious that the sexual drives I was feeling were not going to go away and this was a serious problem for me.

Social connectivity is usually the way to develop sexual intimacy. But as far as I was concerned, being social was sufficiently difficult that to also include sexual intimacy with someone was completely out of the question. Furthermore, that sexual intimacy might involve someone of the same sex was impossible for me to even contemplate, especially after years of being bullied by other males.

Perhaps my state of mind at the time can best be illustrated with a simple analogy that I am shamelessly adapting from the well-known movie, *Big*, starring Tom Hanks. What if a boy in middle school somehow left his body and was suddenly transported into the body of a nineteen-year-old male? How would this boy socially and sexually cope with such an abrupt change? First, he would surely feel uncomfortable in his newly acquired adult body. Second, he would have problems being socially conversant with other nineteen-year-olds on a peer-to-peer level. Third, the normal sexual drives of a nineteen-year-old would be overwhelming for him. Similar to the character in *Big*, at nineteen years old, I felt like an overgrown kid who was outwardly trying his hardest to become an adult because that's what was expected of him, yet inside was stuck in his childhood because that's where he felt the most comfortable.

Aside from feeling immature, the most immediate problem I faced was my sexual identity. Being gay was completely unacceptable to me and made me feel suicidal. I knew I badly needed help. I felt I could no longer keep hiding fears about my sexual orientation from my parents. They deserved to know what a horrible son they had and it was my duty to inform them. Of course, delivering this news in person wasn't possible because of my fragile state. So I decided to write them a letter and hand deliver it when I came home the next weekend.

I will never forget that night. With tears in my eyes, I gave the letter to my dad and then I went on a long drive because I didn't want to be in the house while he was reading it. As I now read the letter, I look back on who I was at that time with sadness and empathy. I'd like to quote portions from it to provide further insight into my psychological state at the time.

Dear Mom and Dad,

What I am about to tell you in this letter is probably going to be the hardest thing that I have ever had to do in my life... What I regretfully have to tell you is that I think I am gay. I am dreadfully scared that this is going to change our relationship drastically... So many times I just wish I could be different and not be this way. I don't want you to view me as inferior. I want our relationship to be the same as it was before... What I am planning to do is not have any relationships with anyone during my life. I refuse to be part of a group that is looked down upon so much, that certain people wished we were dead. I just refuse to partake in this behavior... I feel rejected by the rest of society for being born a certain way. I feel like society hates me for having a certain glitch that I have no control over... Am I really that bad, Mom and Dad? Am I really that inferior? Am I someone even worthy of living? These questions are so confusing to me, because I honestly don't know the answers to them.

When I returned to the house after my dad had finished reading the letter, he hugged me with unconditional acceptance and love. So did my mom. As we began to discuss the content of the letter, they asked me a question I had asked myself many times. How did I know for sure that I was gay? If I had never even kissed anyone of the same or the opposite sex, what real proof did I have? Hearing them pose these questions, I felt a burden lift from my shoulders. My parents and I were on the same wavelength! This was exactly what I had wanted them to say. Maybe it was as simple as just needing some experience with the opposite sex to flip on the heterosexual switch and my problems would be solved.

At the time, if I had to choose between being gay or straight, there was no contest. I wanted to be straight. My parents also wanted me to be straight, not because they were homophobic or prejudiced against gay people, but because I already had a full plate of problems and enough obstacles to overcome.

After further discussion with my parents, we all decided it made sense to get more information from a knowledgeable, objective source to put the question to rest. My parents did some research and found a sex researcher and therapist, Dr Renee Swanson, who also taught at the University of Michigan. She had an excellent reputation in the field of human sexuality. I hoped that she would help settle the score on this pivotal issue and we eagerly made an appointment to go see her. Maybe she could tell me that I wasn't one of those "disgusting" people my philosophy professor had described.

Dr Swanson met us in her office but she wasn't at all what I expected. Instead of being a formal and scholarly woman, she was super-friendly, upbeat, and gregarious. She immediately put my parents and me at ease. On her wall I noticed she had a framed diploma signifying her completion of a seminar at the Kinsey Institute. This immediately caught my attention.

"You studied under Alfred Kinsey?" I asked.

"Not directly," she said. "He's been gone for a long time, but he was a great man and helped a lot of people." This statement contradicted what my professor had said with such certainty. I was confused, but there was a more important issue at hand to be discussed with her.

I then told Dr Swanson why I had come to see her. I talked about the feelings and attractions I had, and then asked her directly if she thought I was gay. In response, she wanted to know how much sexual experience I had had.

"What do you mean by experience?"

"Have you dated any girls?"

"No."

"Well what about guys?"

"No."

"Let me tell you something, honeybun. The proof is in the pudding. How can you know what you want if you haven't tried it yet? You gotta get out there and experiment. Then you'll know. It'll just come naturally."

My parents and I breathed a collective sigh of relief. Dr Swanson had validated what we had previously discussed. That until I had some real experience, I wouldn't know for sure. It was almost as if she was telepathic and told me exactly what I wanted to hear, and it couldn't have come from a more credible source. The verdict was in from a respected expert in human sexuality at the University of Michigan. I wasn't necessarily gay. Hooray and hallelujah!

The only bad news was that if I was ever going to figure out my sexual orientation, I would have to experiment. That statement didn't get any hallelujahs from me, but for the time being my sexual identity crisis was put on hold. The mystery would remain a mystery. I just needed a little more time to sort out my sexuality. Fourteen years to be exact.

With that crisis more or less behind me, I could now focus my attention where it needed to be—on tennis. The winter-spring season would soon be starting, which meant that I couldn't keep going home every weekend. The days of risking my life braving the cold and snowy roads were over. No more hymns to freedom on Fridays and no more traumatizing separations on Sundays. If I was going to play on the tennis team, which I very much wanted to do, I was going to have to sacrifice those weekends at home. Tennis was all I had as far as a positive identity, and I wasn't ready to give that up. So in early February, I started to go through the difficult transition of staying on campus and concentrating on getting ready to play on the tennis team.

The first few weekends of not going home were excruciatingly painful. It was like going through a withdrawal. I sorely missed my parents, since they were my only source of support, but tryouts for the team were on the horizon and, just like in high school, I wanted to play number one singles. The competition was fierce. Grand Valley State University is a Division II NCAA school that has about twenty thousand students. It competes against other colleges that have very competitive athletic teams. I had to beat many other excellent players in the preseason challenge matches to earn the coveted number one singles slot. And I did.

Looking back, it was a miracle that I was able to play the top position. With the extra pounds I had put on, all of my adjustment issues, and the emotional and sexual turmoil I was going through, not to mention keeping up with my studies, I'm amazed I had the energy to focus on tennis. Even more incredible, I finished the tennis season winning far more matches than I lost. One week I was even named "athlete of the week" at Grand Valley and was featured on the local PBS station for a news story where my coach was interviewed and bragged about me. My coach's praise helped boost my ego during those tough times.

Though the season was rewarding, it was also very challenging. One weekend, the team traveled down to Hilton Head Island, South Carolina for a tournament. Every night after the matches were played, the guys on the team headed down to the bars or dance clubs. I stayed at the hotel by myself because I had no desire to socialize with them or to drink. I also felt as if I had nothing in common with my teammates. I did have certain sexual stirrings towards some of them but I tried denying that those feelings carried any significance, because of what Dr Swanson had told me.

Overall, the tennis season, as in high school, had its share of highs and lows. For the most part, I managed to play excellent tennis, but I never socialized with any of my teammates. All I could think about at the last tournament of the season was going to Los Angeles to see *The Price Is Right*.

I have to hand it to my dad. I had my doubts as to whether he had made that promise just to keep me in school and if he would actually follow through on it. But he was a man of his word and our plan was to leave for Los Angeles two days after school ended. I was fixated on the fantasy of attending a game show that I had been watching since the age of three. For me, the prospect was dizzying and exhilarating, like going from San Quentin prison to Willy Wonka's chocolate factory in the span of two days.

In preparation for the trip, I read on the internet that the producers of the show interview every person who comes into the studio for about a minute, because each member of the audience is a potential contestant. I decided I wanted to stand out in a big way so I made a special T-shirt for the occasion so the producers would notice me. On the T-shirt was a picture of the legendary host, Bob Barker, with five of his catchphrases, the most famous being: "Don't forget to have your pets spayed and neutered."

The picture I used on the T-shirt was originally sent to me in response to a fan letter I wrote to Mr Barker around the age of seven or eight. This T-shirt apparently was my golden ticket because at the beginning of the show, Rod Roddy, the announcer of the program, called out, "Nicolas Dubin, come on down," and before I knew it, I was on national television bidding on various merchandise. I eventually got up on stage by winning a recycling cabinet. Once on stage with Mr Barker, I won five thousand dollars in prize money and one thousand dollars in merchandise. But the real thrill wasn't winning the money or the merchandise. It was meeting Bob Barker who had been one of my idols for as long as I could remember. He chuckled as he read his own catchphrases on my T-shirt and he even bantered a little with me on stage. It was an out-of-body experience and it couldn't have come at a better time. Being on *The Price Is Right* was a reward for having endured an excruciatingly difficult year.

With that surreal and uplifting experience behind me, I now had a big decision to make. Would I stay at Grand Valley and play on the tennis team for another year or would I come home and attend a local university? If I came home, I would have to forgo playing tennis on a college team. Since tennis was the only source of a positive identity I had, it was a very difficult decision. As much as I hated being at Grand Valley, I was torn about what to do. Fortunately, over the summer I met someone who shed some much-needed wisdom on my dilemma and helped me come to the right decision for myself.

CHAPTER 6

Undergraduate Years

What Should I Be When I Grow Up?

In June of 1997, I had been home from Grand Valley for nearly a month, but I still hadn't made a decision about whether to go back the following year. It should have been a no-brainer. I never wanted to spend time at Grand Valley, except for attending classes. Other than playing in tennis tournaments, I drove home almost every weekend to see my parents. I didn't make a single friend. I was depressed during the entire academic year and often felt suicidal. What was there to even think about?

The biggest obstacle in my decision-making was my strong desire not to be viewed by others as a quitter. Of course, this concern was ridiculous, as it was based on the erroneous assumption that anyone else cared about or even noticed what I chose to do. As I contemplated whether to return for my sophomore year or stay at home, I was denying my real emotional needs and making my top priority what I assumed others would think of me, just like I did in my senior year when making my decision to attend Grand Valley.

In my flawed worldview, I thought if I showed any sign of emotional immaturity, others would see me as a failure. Coming home and living with my parents would certainly show the world just how much of a child I really was. It was very important for me to appear normal and to try to hide all of my differences. I had an inferiority complex a mile wide and was always trying to overcompensate for it. That sense of inferiority accounts for why, in the end, playing tennis turned out to be a profoundly unsatisfying experience, with the exception of Tennis Europe. Even my status as a highly ranked tennis player did not help me gain the friendships I was seeking or the true acceptance I was longing for from others.

Unfortunately, at the age of twenty, I still had not developed any kind of self-acceptance or awareness of my strengths and limitations. I had not yet begun to believe in my own inherent goodness and worthiness as a person. This lack of self-acceptance explains why I had to be the best player on every tennis team. Without that awareness, the prospect of not playing college tennis was like giving up my entire identity. All of my past accomplishments were, in some way or another, related to tennis. Not returning to Grand Valley meant the end of my tennis career at the ripe old age of twenty—a sure sign that others would judge me as a loser. No matter how many times my parents and I discussed the various pros and cons of my decision, I remained stuck. I needed someone to step in and be the voice of reason.

Unbeknownst to me, while I was attending Grand Valley, my parents were receiving counseling from a therapist named Julia Press. She was helping them cope with the ongoing crisis of my being away at college. They felt that meeting Julia might benefit me by providing clarity as I made this important decision. I was surprised and a little angry that my parents had, without my permission, been sharing all of my dark secrets with someone I had never met. As frustrated as I was by this sense of betrayal, I felt compelled to meet her because I knew I needed all the help I could get.

In spite of my apprehension about meeting her, Julia turned out to be a beautiful human being. There are very few people who I feel truly understand me but Julia has always been one of them. To this day, she remains one of the most important and supportive people in my life. When I first met her, I immediately felt that she understood me perfectly. She also had the good sense to challenge some of my irrational beliefs. I began our meeting by telling her that if I came home, I would be perceived as a loser, a failure, and a quitter in the eyes of everyone I knew. Julia patiently explained that this voice was my own inner critic speaking. She stated that I had a right and a responsibility to make a decision that took my own needs into account, as opposed to the false, imagined needs or expectations of others. Her statement was a wake-up call. For the first time in my life, I could see that I had a compulsive need to earn the approval of others. Julia's wise words reminded me that my sanity was more important than winning any tennis match. That day, after talking with Julia, I decided to move back home and attend Oakland University, which did not have a tennis team, but was only a fifteen-minute drive from my house.

During the next three-and-a-half years, my life primarily consisted of going to classes and coming back home. My social life was nonexistent with the exception of playing an occasional tennis game with someone. I still relied on my parents almost exclusively for company. My life was quite boring and routine, which was fine with me after the previous year of intense chaos and confusion.

In my sophomore year, I began seriously weighing up my career options for the first time. I realized I didn't have any real skills other than playing tennis. But I remembered how much joy I got from doing the high school announcements and thought it would be cool if I could earn a living working in the field of broadcasting. Clearly, my dream of replacing Bob Barker as the next host of *The Price Is Right* was a fantasy. So I turned my attention towards what I thought was a more realistic goal—being a radio DJ. I decided to major in communications and applied to the student radio station to see if I could host a weekly program.

When I met the student manager of the radio station, he told me I needed to make an audition tape in order to be considered. This was just a formality but I took the assignment very seriously. He explained the station format was one in which all of the music had to be the type you would not hear on regular commercial radio. This format requirement posed a problem for me because my level of musical sophistication did not go much beyond my favorite artists. I wasn't really knowledgeable about any particular genre of music such as reggae, classical, electronics, or bluegrass. The only type of music that seemed workable for me was jazz. My father had always loved jazz music and had taken me to see a number of renowned jazz artists. I liked jazz but was certainly not an aficionado. I didn't know much about this type of music, but that was about to change in a hurry. I was ready to aim my laser-like ability to focus on the subject of jazz music.

As I started to immerse myself in jazz, it soon became clear who my best friends in life were going to be. They were not people with whom I could have real relationships, but rather the glorious sounds of jazz musicians whose music offered me a safe haven from the complexities and harshness of the world. I decided to take the five thousand dollars I won on *The Price Is Right* and spend it all on jazz CDs. I also read everything I could find on all the jazz greats. Beyond becoming highly knowledgeable about jazz, I developed a love affair with the music. My fascination with jazz became a full-blown special interest. I even got to the point where I could recognize various jazz musicians upon hearing only the first few bars of a song, a skill usually reserved for trained musicians.

My love of jazz led me to *The Great American Songbook*, a collection of songs from the days of Tin Pan Alley through the 1960s. These songs are also referred to as "standards" because they are considered classics. Almost all of the great jazz musicians performed standards. My knowledge of these songs became all encompassing. To this day, I can usually identify almost any standard as well as who wrote it and what jazz instrumentalists or singers had at one time or another recorded it.

It is ironic that most of my favorite songs are standards. These songs usually center on themes of love, heartbreak, longing, and connectedness—the very emotions I have not yet personally experienced in a romantic context. Perhaps, I have vicariously experienced some of those emotions through these beautiful songs.

My weekly radio show was a complete joy for me. I called my program "Straight, No Chaser," after a Thelonious Monk song, because I thought the title sounded hip. At the time, I didn't have any idea what the title actually meant since I have never had a drink in my life. Part of the reason I loved doing my show was because it required a minimal amount of social interaction. I liked the fact that I was alone in a little studio. It was the perfect college activity for someone with Asperger's because it did not involve socializing with other people. But I loved it for an even more significant reason. I was playing music that I considered to be an extension of myself. As a DJ, I gravitated towards playing those jazz musicians whose music I felt best expressed my true musical taste. Hosting this program gave me the opportunity to be totally authentic about something that genuinely interested me rather than worrying about how others would perceive me.

In my sophomore year of college, I wrote a letter to a DJ named Pete, who hosted a jazz show on a local public radio station. This was my way of trying to make a contact in the radio business. I wanted to see if Pete could use my help in any way. Pete had been the musical director of a jazz festival in Detroit for many years and had met many of the greatest jazz musicians of all time. I loved listening to his program and felt that we shared similar musical tastes. I hoped I would at least get a chance to meet him.

Pete wrote back right away and suggested we meet. I had no work resume other than my tennis jobs. All I had going for me was my passion for and knowledge of jazz. I was extremely nervous when I first met Pete because I didn't want to appear socially awkward, but he seemed to like me right away. He was impressed that I knew so much about jazz at such a young age and asked me if I would be willing to distribute flyers for him at college campuses throughout the state for a jazz and blues festival he ran every summer. Of course, no pay was involved but I considered it an honor and a privilege to assist him.

Soon I began spending most of my Saturday nights with Pete while he did his radio show. It was a great experience for me, fetching CDs for him from the enormous music library at the station. From seven to ten, he and I were the only two people in the studio and it felt as if we owned the place. I soon learned that this was not a typical broadcasting environment and that if I were to go into radio, I would have to interact with a lot more people. Pete also told me that being a DJ paid very little. Although I wasn't happy to hear that, I was undeterred. Broadcasting was still my goal.

Sadly, my hopes of pursuing a career in broadcasting were soon to be dashed. One of the professors at Oakland University who supervised the student DJs told me I would never make it in radio because my voice was too high. I never questioned the truth of what he was telling me. I was crushed by his comment because I had invested so much of myself in the dream of working in this field.

Thereafter, a friend of my parents arranged for me to interview for an internship at Marianne Williamson's national radio program, which at the time originated in Detroit. Marianne Williamson, a brilliant and well-known spiritual leader with a huge following, became famous for her bestselling book, *A Return to Love*, as well as through her appearances on *The Oprah Winfrey Show*. I had attended a few of her lectures and was very impressed by her remarkable speaking skills and her approach to spirituality.

I was nervous because this was my first job interview; all of my tennis jobs had simply been offered to me. I knew the interview wasn't going to be easy, but I considered it a challenge and went into it with an open mind. However, when I got to the station, I was in for a rude awakening. It was not at all like the low-key atmosphere with Pete at the radio station. In contrast, this studio was a noisy, hustle-bustle, high-octane environment. Working there would require intense socializing and continuous multitasking, both of which are major weaknesses for me. I could tell right away by the tightness in my chest that I couldn't do this job, but I never had to because they didn't offer it to me. To this day, I'll never forget the initial feeling I had when I stepped inside that hectic radio station. In that moment, I had a clear realization: radio and I were not a good fit. But it was a little too late. I had majored in communications for the past two years and there was nothing else I could think of to do.

There was another option my parents were encouraging me to pursue but I was dead set against it. They felt that teaching tennis would be a good way to earn a living in the future. I had already been teaching tennis part time at different clubs since high school, but I was horrible at it. I was a good tennis player but not a good teacher. I knew this for a fact, but there was no way to convince my parents otherwise without starting an argument. They pressured me to take the test to become a certified tennis professional, which I did. Today, my parents say the reason they kept pushing this idea was that tennis was my only interest at the time other than music. This was true. I had not yet blossomed as a student and in fact struggled with many of my undergraduate classes outside of my major.

Although I was opposed to a career as a tennis pro, I still took part-time tennis jobs while completing my undergraduate degree. In my sophomore year of college, a tennis friend, who was now the varsity coach of the team where I went to high school, asked me to be the junior varsity coach. I reluctantly took the position because I didn't have any other job opportunities at the time. There was also a part of me that didn't want my tennis days to be completely over and I saw coaching as a way to continue my involvement in the sport. In an interesting twist, I would be coaching at the same high school where I had been a social pariah. In a way it felt good to go back to the place where I had felt so powerless but would now be in a position of authority.

As it turned out, taking the job was a huge mistake. From the first day, I knew I was in trouble because I had the same tightness in my chest that I had experienced at the Marianne Williamson show, only it was much more intense. I wanted so badly to quit but I had already signed a contract. What had I gotten myself into?

The primary reason the job proved to be so difficult was that every day when I looked at those ninth and tenth grade boys, I saw my former tormenters. As a result, I found myself intimidated by them and seeking their approval. Because of this dynamic, I lost all authority as a coach and became immobilized. The practices were downright anarchistic and the players ran all over me. Many of them chose to skip practice and I felt powerless to do anything about it. I was scared that my own players would bully me if I confronted them. Here I was, a coach who was afraid of his own players, but in retrospect it makes perfect sense. I may have only been a few years older than these players, but the truth was I felt emotionally younger than them.

An example of my immaturity as a coach took place when a couple of my players asked me whom I had dated in high school. I lied and gave the name of a girl who perhaps some of them knew. Telling this lie was stupid and childish because it could have easily backfired on me. It just shows the lengths I would go to in order to create the appearance of normalcy and to hide my sexual confusion.

I only lasted one year at this job. I ask myself now why I didn't listen to the inner voice that told me I was stepping into a hornets' nest by taking this position. I should have known that working with a group of boys who were the same age as the boys who used to bully me was a recipe for disaster. Once again, I didn't listen to myself. I ignored my instincts, the tightness in my chest, and my past experiences.

I continued to take other jobs teaching tennis with similar results, but the same problem kept cropping up over and over again: I felt like a child who was playing the part of an authority figure. Paradoxically, the more I tried to act like an adult to compensate for my insecurities, the more immature my actions became. For example, I was teaching at a private club and one day I bought a bullhorn because I thought it would help me assert more authority. My reasoning was if the kids weren't going to listen to my directions with my normal speaking voice, perhaps my amplified voice would do the trick. Did I ask my boss permission to do this? The thought never crossed my mind. Needless to say, he was horrified by this tactic and told me to immediately throw the bullhorn in the trash. He said this was a country club, not the Notre Dame Fighting Irish football team.

On another occasion, it was my job to unlock the main clubhouse door in the morning. I was the only pro there that day with the key. With my notoriously poor fine motor skills I was having great difficulty opening the door. There were two junior teams eagerly waiting to get in. The longer I struggled with the key and the longer they waited, the more humiliating the situation became for me. Finally, I asked one of the twelve-year-olds to try to open the door, which he was able to do in a matter of seconds. The kids erupted in laughter, which of course was all too familiar to me.

Aside from exploring two career paths that were dead ends, the most disconcerting thing about my three-and-a-half years at Oakland University, was that my sexuality went completely underground. My parents and I never discussed the subject during that time. Talk about the elephant in the room. The only time the subject came up was when my parents put pressure on me to start dating. Usually, I would just respond with a quick, "I'm not ready for that yet," and the discussion would end without further comment. Neither my parents nor I ever brought up the possibility of me being gay again, until many years after our meeting with Dr Swanson. Essentially, I went back into the closet.

As I headed towards graduation, I realized how emotionally and sexually arrested I was for my age. Feeling like a child in an adult's body made it impossible for me to understand and explore my sexuality. I thought perhaps my delayed social and sexual development was making me feel I might be gay. The bottom line was that my sexuality was totally baffling to me.

Career concerns, for the moment, helped me to postpone dealing with my sexual confusion. I was about to graduate from college without any inkling of what I wanted to do. I was at a crossroads and needed to grow up fast. I was no longer a child. I was now a college graduate. How would I respond to this drastic life change? Would I continue to teach tennis as a career, go back to radio, or would something else I had never even considered present itself to me?

CHAPTER 7
Master's Degree and Dating

Dead Ends

For as long as I can recall, I have never enjoyed my birthday. Not because I didn't like receiving presents, but because I always felt much younger than others my age, and my actual birthday was a harsh reminder of that gap. Turning twenty-three was no different. I was adrift in all aspects of my life. I had graduated from college with a degree in communications, but I still had no idea of what kind of work I was going to do. Having already ruled out broadcasting and tennis, I needed inspiration and direction, but no job seemed to fit my limited set of skills. From time to time, I would hear about people my age who were going to law and medical school or were already working as stockbrokers, accountants, and journalists. They were successful and I wanted to be successful too.

Besides my lack of career direction, my parents were putting more pressure on me to start dating. Up until this point, I never had any willingness or desire to do so. But after I graduated college in 2000, I began to hear about some former high school classmates who were getting engaged. Even a cousin, who I later learned was diagnosed with Asperger's and who had never dated before, suddenly had a girlfriend. His brother, who was only a few years older than I and to whom I always negatively compared myself, was married, had a career, and would soon be starting a family. As one might imagine, I was jealous of these family members and former classmates. I wanted what they had, not because I had always dreamed of being a husband or a father, but because I wanted to feel my age. Being married and having kids would prove to others, once and for all, that I had really grown up. My pattern of needing the approval of others was clearly repeating itself. I still wanted to be like everyone else the same way I did when I chose to go away to Grand Valley even though my instincts told me it wasn't in my best interest.

As I was evaluating my career options post-graduation, I made a decision to put dating, relationships, and my sexuality on hold. Dealing with my career was all I could focus on at that time. Fortunately, one particular experience significantly helped me to identify what I wanted to do. Soon after I graduated college, I attended a lecture given by Jonathan Mooney, a disabilities advocate, who grew up with severe learning disabilities. In spite of his challenges, he managed to become a very successful author and workshop presenter. Mooney's speech was transformative for me. His enthusiasm and sense of purpose were palpable. He cared about individuals who had suffered throughout life because they were misunderstood. He wanted to help their plight as adults. I walked out of that auditorium feeling a kinship with Mooney's altruistic mission. For the first time in my life, I felt called to explore a career that focused on something other than me. With radio, I wanted to be heard. With tennis, I wanted to be validated for a skill. Now, in addition to those two goals, I also wanted to do something to help others. I wanted to make a difference.

With a newfound passion to help the disabilities community, I decided to apply for a master's degree in special education at the University of Detroit Mercy. To my amazement, I was accepted into the program. That I was now in graduate school was surprising since I had never taken academic studies that seriously. Now I was in it for the long haul to become a special education teacher. Having a goal-oriented outlook about my future made me feel more like an adult. My professional priorities were now in check and I began to read all I could about this new field I would soon be entering. Although I was intellectually starting to blossom, socially and sexually, things were quite different.

After my tumultuous year at Grand Valley, I had moved back home while I attended Oakland University. My parents understood my need to live with them, but after I graduated they started encouraging me to think about getting my own apartment. They felt that living on my own would help me to separate emotionally from them and to become a more independent person. We discussed this idea for almost a year but I was petrified at the prospect of leaving home.

With a lot of support from my parents and from Julia, our family counselor, I finally moved out of the house on August 11, 2001, and into an apartment about five miles away from my parents' house. Considering the enormous amount of anxiety I felt, my apartment might as well have been in China. Living apart from my parents was extremely difficult for me because I still felt as if I needed them in so many ways. For example, my parents were paying my rent and otherwise supporting me financially. Even though I had made progress intellectually, other areas of growth were still lagging far behind.

Consequently, a huge schism formed between my intellectual development and my social and sexual development. I was taking graduate level courses, but at the same time I was visiting my parents almost every day. I relished writing complex, scholarly papers, but I felt socially inept if I had to engage in a five-minute conversation with one of my classmates. I had no problem sitting through three-hour lectures, but I would have a meltdown if someone unexpectedly called me on the phone or was more than five minutes late to meet me somewhere.

During the three-and-a-half years I spent at the University of Detroit Mercy, I breezed through most of my classes and got As in almost all of them. I enjoyed learning about the theories of developmental psychologists like Howard Gardner, Jean Piaget, and Lawrence Kohlberg. I also gained a better appreciation and understanding of learning disabilities because of their personal relevance to my life. Classes with a more practical component were not as appealing to me. I had no desire to learn how to teach social studies or science to elementary school children. Those subjects were out of my range of interests, but somehow I got through them.

The social and sexual aspects of my life had been stagnant for some time, but that was about to change. In one discussion with my dad where he was again encouraging me to date, I told him I wasn't ready because I didn't have any idea how to be physically intimate with a woman. I reminded him that Dr Swanson had said I needed to get some real-life experience in order to discover my sexual orientation. My dad tried explaining to me that knowing how to act sexually tends to come naturally in the moment, but his assurance was meaningless to me. I told him, without first learning how to physically relate to a woman, I wouldn't know what to do in the unlikely event that I became involved in a relationship. I was afraid that without this practical experience, I would make a complete fool of myself. The question was: where could I get this kind of experience?

Sensitive to my dilemma, my dad tried his best to come up with a solution. He even went as far as going on the internet to check out sexual surrogacy. A sexual surrogate is someone who usually works in conjunction with a psychiatrist or psychologist and helps a client, through physical contact, to deal with issues, such as dating anxiety, sexual inhibition, and lack of sexual confidence. My father learned that the use of sexual surrogates was generally not legal. He again suggested I start dating, but given my mountain of insecurities and level of sexual confusion, I continued to resist.

After much thought and research, the only option I could come up with to gain this experience was to go to a legal brothel, which is different from sexual surrogacy. I was desperate and wanted to move forward in learning about my sexuality and feel more confident in starting the dating process. Trust me, I did not feel remotely comfortable with this idea, but in my mind, this less than ideal solution seemed to be the only way I could gain some sexual experience in a safe and non-judgmental environment. Dr Swanson's statement, "the proof is in the pudding," was never far from my mind.

When I approached my father with this idea, he initially reacted negatively. He was rightly concerned with the legality and safety of such an arrangement as well as whether such an experience might be upsetting or even damaging to me. I told him how badly I wanted to do it and that there was no other way. He finally agreed to give it some thought but said he would have to make sure that it would be totally legal and safe. I did more research and found a county in Nevada where brothels were legal, and after much soul searching on both our parts we made the decision to go there. Before we left, he called ahead to specifically request someone who specialized in shy men with no previous sexual experience and made an appointment with someone he was told met that criterion.

I was a nervous wreck leading up to this trip. There was so much riding on it for me. In retrospect, part of my anxiety may have been due to the uncertainty about whether or not I was sexually attracted to women. The truth was, given my extreme social anxiety and sexual inhibitions, being close to anyone female or male would have been terrifying for me.

The experience turned out to be a complete disaster. I felt no connection to the woman my appointment was with. The room we were in was cold and sterile with bright fluorescent lights (an Asperger's nightmare) and a hard linoleum floor. Rather than an intimate or romantic experience, it felt more as though I was there for a medical procedure. The woman who supposedly specialized in shy men was cold and impatient with me. The appointment seemed to last an eternity and ultimately was unsuccessful. I went home devastated.

Looking back, my expectations for this experience were completely unrealistic. I was hopelessly naive and actually believed that after an hour with this woman, all the questions I had about my sexuality would be answered. Since that time, I have been able to put this experience into perspective and have often wondered why some form of sexual surrogacy is not legal so that trained professionals could help people like me become more comfortable with their sexuality. A therapist I know told me that most of his clients with AS have little to no sexual experience and have expressed a desire to have the opportunity to learn how to be sexual with another person in a safe, non-judgmental environment.

The crisis in Nevada intensified my confusion about my sexual orientation. I didn't get the results I wanted, but I wasn't sure anyone could have under such adverse circumstances. After I came home, I was in worse shape than before. The trip did not clarify anything for me. It just made me much more depressed and I began to have suicidal thoughts.

At that point, my parents became concerned and felt I needed to get professional help from a specialist in sexuality. Julia, who I had been working with on and off since Grand Valley, agreed. My parents did some research and found a well-respected psychologist who specialized in sexual issues.

Upon meeting Dr Green, I was immediately impressed with him. Over the years, I had seen other therapists, but most of them seemed to patronize me and would never give me any meaningful feedback. They tended to only mirror back whatever I said to them. Right now I didn't need mirroring. I needed someone to be straight with me. In a nutshell, that was Dr Green. He was smart and a good listener and he told me what he thought.

As my therapy with Dr Green progressed, he quickly observed that I was chronically anxious and depressed. He saw that my adjustment issues were extremely problematic. He felt my dependence on my parents was of great concern. He knew I didn't have any friends and was aware of my periodic suicidal thoughts. In most of our sessions, Dr Green's goal was to help me survive the daily and weekly challenges of my life. Even though my presenting problem was sexual confusion, the increasing demands of my external life seemed to take priority. I have since learned that this dynamic is not uncommon for people with Asperger's who are in therapy. There are so many life issues that need to be addressed and sexuality often gets lost in the shuffle.

In the years since my arrest, I have talked with several therapists who work with Asperger's adults and adolescents. These therapists acknowledged they were reluctant to discuss sex with their clients both because it is such a daunting topic for that population but also because there are so many other pressing issues that always need to be dealt with. Parents of children and young adults with Asperger's are as reluctant to bring up the subject of sex as individuals with Asperger's are themselves. Consequently, the subject of sex has remained in the shadows. This lack of attention to the sexuality of Asperger's individuals needs to change. Research shows that having Asperger's hinders normal sexual development and can create a multitude of problems. The differences in sexual development between people with Asperger's and neurotypicals need to be understood by those who treat Asperger's patients. Unfortunately, there are hardly any psychologists or therapists whose expertise includes both autism and sexuality.

In one of our early sessions, I told Dr Green I believed the real source of my chronic depression was sexual confusion and that perhaps if I got married, I would no longer be depressed. Dr Green disagreed. He didn't think getting married would cure my depression, but I held firm. I still wanted what everyone else seemed to have in life. I wanted Dr Green to tell me that it would be all right for me to start dating even if I wasn't entirely sure it would work out. In spite of my trip to Nevada, I told him, I still wasn't sure whether I was "G.A.Y."

"Nick," said Dr Green. "You can't even say the word. You have to spell it out. Why is it so hard for you to even say that word?" he asked.

"I don't know. You tell me."

He said, "I really want you to think about it."

"All I know is that I want what everyone else has in life: to be married, to have kids, to be a success."

"Hold on," he said. "I know many single people of all ages who have never married and lead very successful lives. They consider themselves happy and fulfilled." Dr Green's response shocked me. Up to this point, I believed only married people could be happy and successful.

"So if I don't get married, I'm not a failure?"

"Absolutely not. How did you come to that conclusion?"

"I guess it's just ingrained in our culture."

"Nick, let me be straight with you, no pun intended. Only you can know for sure if you're gay and I can't tell you because I don't live inside your body. But the fact that you couldn't even say the word gay means something. I'd like you to reflect on the significance of that."

"Okay. Whatever," I said in a defeatist tone.

Although it now seems clear I was gay, I still resisted coming to that conclusion. It took many more years before I was able to come to terms with my sexuality.

I would like to explain my desire at that time not to be gay. I have a first cousin who is gay, my dad's best friend is gay, and my rabbi was gay. There was never a hint of homophobia in our house. However, like many teens who are bullied for being perceived as gay, my experiences caused me to internalize negative messages about homosexuality.

My resistance to being gay at this point during my therapy stemmed more from the fact that it would be another major way in which I was different and, even more significant, it presented an insurmountable obstacle to getting married, having a family and being like everyone else. So, even though I was still confused about my sexuality, my desire to be like everyone else motivated me to start dating.

Like many people today, I found the few dates I had through online dating websites. My first date was with a jazz singer which, given my interests, sounded very promising. I took her to a nice restaurant and brought her a bouquet of roses. I tried to control the flow of conversation by asking her a lot of questions about herself, but didn't disclose any information about me. In hindsight, this one-sided conversation and the fact I brought her roses on our first date probably made her uncomfortable. I called her the next day, but never heard back from her. This pattern repeated itself with at least three or four other women. We would go out, I would call or email the next day, and then if I didn't get an immediate response, I would leave an angry phone message or write an email accusing these women of behaving insensitively towards me. Clearly, my social skills were abysmal.

Just as I was ready to give up on dating for good, I met a woman on a Jewish dating website who was also studying to be a teacher, so we had at least two things in common: being Jewish and our careers. We didn't really click and I never felt physically attracted to her, but nevertheless we went out for about two months. She actually seemed to like me at the beginning, although there were definite problems between us. Once when we were at a movie theatre, she tried holding my hand and I tensed up and pulled away. I'm sure in that moment she felt I was rejecting her. Another time, she surprised me by coming over to my apartment unannounced. I told her how inconsiderate she was in not giving me any advance notice. She left my apartment very angry. She was also frustrated that I preferred to communicate through email and not talk on the phone, something that to this day I find difficult. The last straw for her was when she invited me to a close friend's wedding and I didn't know how to dance and had trouble socializing with her friends. The next day, she dumped me. I felt both rejected and relieved.

Around the same time she broke up with me I began student teaching, which I needed to pass to obtain my teaching certificate. In order to become a special education teacher, I had to complete two semesters of student teaching: one in a regular second grade classroom and the other in a special education center. These two student teaching assignments were literally the last leg of my three-and-a-half year master's degree journey.

Over the summer, I told the special education teacher at the elementary school where I would be student teaching in the fall that I had concerns about my poor handwriting. She generously agreed to work with me over the summer to show me the correct way to hold a pencil, to print longhand, and to write cursive. For several months, I spent three days a week at her house working on a skill that I didn't need to learn but for teaching, since I did all my written work on a computer. Having such terrible handwriting should have been a major clue right from the start that I was headed into a disastrous situation. If I had to teach a skill to second-graders that I could barely perform myself, something was very wrong.

Once I started student teaching, many problems other than my handwriting quickly emerged. I didn't know how to relate to children and I had trouble being an authority figure around them. Disciplining a student was almost impossible for me. I also saw that multitasking was an essential skill for this job that I didn't have. I was completely overwhelmed by the number of tasks I needed to perform each day and things began to slip through the cracks.

The second grade teacher I worked under grew very impatient with me. In spite of the handwriting help I had received over the summer, I still couldn't write legibly on the blackboard. The children teased me that they had better handwriting than I did. But handwriting was the least of my problems. One day I broke the school's costly laminating machine. I was constantly forgetting to perform tasks I had been asked to do. I had no interest in the different subjects I was teaching. At lunch, I always left school to avoid having to socialize with the children or the teachers. I later learned the teaching staff frowned upon my lack of socializing with them.

The situation grew worse every day. Nothing I was doing was right and there wasn't anything I liked about the job. I was also afraid that if I had this much trouble teaching second grade, my problems would only intensify with special education students. Initially the idea of being a special education teacher seemed appealing because I wanted to help others who suffered as I had. But I had not thought through this decision and once again I had ignored my legitimate limitations and needs. After only four weeks, it was clear I could not handle this job.

The principal, the second grade teacher, and my university supervisor all politely told me that the situation wasn't working out and strongly suggested I consider other options. My university supervisor assured me I would still graduate with a master's degree in special education because I had completed all the coursework, but that I would not be a state certified teacher. In one respect, this was a relief because I now realized I didn't really want to be an elementary school teacher. But in another respect, this failure to complete student teaching was more devastating than anything that had ever happened to me. I had lost my purpose in life. With my career and my attempts at dating both over, I felt as if my life was not worth living.

CHAPTER 8

Diagnosis Asperger's

A New Beginning

Sigmund Freud said that the two most important things in life are work and love, and I had just failed miserably at both of them. At age twenty-six, I was now standing on the sidelines watching the world pass me by like a parade. Relationships seemed out of the question, finding purposeful work looked hopeless, and my sexual confusion was ever-present in the midst of all this other turmoil. After the abrupt end of student teaching, I was so depressed I didn't leave my apartment for months, other than to visit my parents. Some days, doing anything like shopping for groceries or even taking a shower, required more energy than I could summon.

In the midst of this severe depression, I was diagnosed with type 2 diabetes, which was probably a result of the binge eating that had started at Grand Valley as a way to cope with my anxiety and depression. My parents were frustrated and angry with me for not taking better physical care of myself over the years. Their anger added to my guilt, but as crazy as it sounds, there was a part of me that was relieved to have a medical condition that actually might shorten my life. I had always been petrified at the thought of growing old without my parents being around to help support me in numerous ways. My thinking was if they outlived me, it wouldn't be such a terrible thing. Even though I was in therapy with Dr Green and under the watch of a psychiatrist who had been prescribing medication since my year at Grand Valley, life seemed totally futile.

I felt I had two choices: give up or fight back. After months of staying in my apartment and feeling completely paralyzed, I finally chose the latter. I knew if I was going to go on living, something had to change. I needed to find out, once and for all, why I always struggled so much in life. My learning disabilities were not a sufficient explanation for all my differences and difficulties in life. There had to be more of a reason for what caused my social isolation, my need for strict routine, my intolerance of change, my chronic anxiety and depression, and my sexual confusion. I also needed to know how I could graduate with a master's degree in special education (magna cum laude) and still fail so miserably at student teaching.

In an effort to get answers to some of these questions, I turned to the self-help and psychology sections of various bookstores. I read about many different diagnoses and found I could relate to some of them but none could fully explain all my deficits. Depression could provide reasons for periods of withdrawal, but it did not address my auditory sensitivities or why I engaged in repetitive behaviors. Anxiety was certainly the origin for my compulsive personality traits, but it didn't account for my social and emotional immaturity. Post-traumatic stress disorder brought forth insights from having been bullied and sexually humiliated in middle school, but it couldn't help me understand neurological behaviors that were present long before middle school, like jumping and flapping my arms as a toddler. After several months, I became frustrated that I couldn't find anything in these books that offered a coherent explanation for why I was the way I was.

At the same time I was trying to get at the root of my problems, the pressure to find a new career felt like a thousand-pound weight pressing on my shoulders. One thing I knew for sure: I wasn't ready for the workplace. I needed to go back to school, if for nothing else than to further delay having to look for employment. But I felt stymied. I didn't want to make another mistake. What kind of graduate program would be right for me?

In looking for clues as to what subject I might pursue, I remembered that I particularly enjoyed the classes I took towards my master's degree that had a psychological or theoretical component. Also, since I had attended Jonathan Mooney's speech a few years earlier, insight into the human condition had become more meaningful to me, as had my desire to help others. Based on these rather limited reasons, I decided to apply to a doctoral program at the Michigan School of Professional Psychology.

During my interview, the president of the school asked me to explain why I didn't finish my student teaching requirement. I think she was concerned that I might not be sufficiently committed to complete the four-year doctoral program. I simply told her that during student teaching I had discovered that being an elementary school teacher was not the right career choice for me. After the interview, I had serious doubts about whether I would be admitted. To my astonishment I was accepted into the program on the condition that I pass several undergraduate courses in psychology that were prerequisites for admission.

One of those required courses was abnormal psychology. This class became pivotal in my ongoing search for an explanation of why I was so different from other people. One day in class, I read about a diagnosis I was only vaguely familiar with—Asperger's syndrome. As I read the description provided in my textbook, my jaw dropped. Asperger's seemed to accurately define who I was and the deficits I had experienced throughout my life. My only reservation was a reference to this diagnosis being on the autism spectrum. Then I remembered being called "Rain Man" at the Oberlin tennis camp. Was there something prophetic about that? Maybe the person who called me that name was actually being observant. For the first time, I strongly considered the possibility that I was autistic.

Shortly thereafter, I was in a bookstore and picked up a book on Asperger's written by my esteemed co-author, Dr Tony Attwood. This book literally saved my life. I felt as if I was reading a point-by-point description of my personality as well as an explanation for all the difficulties in my life. Dr Attwood also highlighted the many strengths, gifts, and talents that people with Asperger's have, including the tendency to develop and focus on special interests. I completely identified with this trait through my consuming interests in game shows, tennis, and jazz. At age twenty-seven, I finally found the answer I was looking for!

I was excited to share this major discovery with my parents because I assumed they would share in my enthusiasm. That was not the case. Both of them resisted the notion that I could be autistic. They were also concerned that having a label connected to autism would limit the way others might view me as well as the way I might view myself. Undeterred, I passionately argued my case and provided evidence from different books for my parents to read. I was so convinced that I insisted on getting an evaluation from a neuropsychologist. Finally, my mom and dad agreed.

After doing a lot of research, my parents found a reputable neuropsychologist, Dr Sheldrake, with a specialty in autism spectrum disorders and made an appointment for me to be evaluated. This evaluation took several days, which included giving me a battery of tests. A week later my parents and I reconvened to meet with Dr Sheldrake to hear his conclusions. The verdict was in. I unequivocally had Asperger's syndrome. Cue the Hallelujah Chorus from Handel's *Messiah*!

Though my parents had initially resisted the idea that I had autism, they were visibly relieved to finally have an explanation for so many of my life's struggles. All three of us were incredibly grateful to have the answer we had been seeking for so long. I was no longer the enigma I thought I was. There was a reason I failed student teaching, a reason I couldn't adapt to going away to college, a reason I couldn't open the classroom door in second grade, a reason I was such an easy target for bullies, a reason I felt like a child in an adult's body, a reason I had not started dating, and a reason I felt so different from everyone else.

In addition to being diagnosed with Asperger's, Dr Sheldrake also identified me as having a nonverbal learning disability. A nonverbal learning disability is quite common among individuals with Asperger's and signifies a large gap between one's verbal and performance IQs. Verbally, I function at a very high level, but on performance tasks relating to visual spatial processing such as tying a tie or perceiving shapes and replicating them on paper, I am severely impaired. Dr Sheldrake found that my performance IQ was four standard deviations below my verbal IQ. This score reflects how my ability to pick up on social cues and form relationships is severely hindered.

After going over all his findings with us, Dr Sheldrake expressed some concern about my working towards a doctoral degree in psychology and ultimately becoming a psychotherapist. He felt this career was not consistent with my strengths and weaknesses. He explained that psychotherapy involves participating in an intimate relationship between therapist and client and that this type of work could prove emotionally depleting for me. Since I had already been accepted into the program, his concern presented a major dilemma for me.

"So if I don't pursue this program, what would I do then?" I asked Dr Sheldrake.

"Well, what is it you want to do?" he asked me.

Suddenly the answer came to me, almost without having to think about it.

"I want to help others with Asperger's," I said. "I want my degree in psychology to enhance my ability to help those on the autism spectrum in whatever way I can."

"I think I can help you accomplish that goal," Dr Sheldrake said, "but you don't have to drop out of this new program because of your diagnosis. If anything, the diagnosis seems to have given you a new sense of purpose in life. In my report, I'm going to recommend that your school make some simple accommodations, which will help you achieve your goal of assisting others on the autism spectrum. Nick, I believe you're someone who will be extremely beneficial to that community. You majored in communications. You're articulate. You will be able to translate to parents, teachers, and therapists who work with people on the spectrum what it's really like to live with Asperger's, both as an expert and as someone with real-life experience."

I didn't know it then, but he was mapping out my future.

After receiving the diagnosis, I was now in a strange position. I had been accepted into a doctoral program but the admissions committee didn't know I had Asperger's. I felt as though I needed to let the school know about this new development to see if they would permit me to stay in the program and if they would be willing to accept the accommodations Dr Sheldrake had recommended.

I made an appointment with the admissions committee and took Dr Sheldrake's written report with me. I was scared. I wanted to be totally honest and not start the program without first disclosing my diagnosis. I told the committee I had not received the diagnosis prior to my acceptance and that I now realized becoming a psychotherapist was not the right career for me. I then outlined how I thought a doctoral degree could further my professional goals. I highlighted passages in Dr Sheldrake's report where he suggested some accommodations, such as having non-clinical internships and not applying for licensure. In every other way, I would complete the same coursework required of every other student, including the writing of a dissertation. I pled my case and the members of the committee saw my intentions were sincere.

Initially, they seemed skeptical, but after a few days of deliberation, I received a call from the president of the school. She said my request for accommodations had been granted and the school was delighted to have me as a student. I couldn't have been happier. With these minimal accommodations in place, my path was laid out before me.

Now all my time and energy went into my studies, but as a consequence my sexual issues remained underground. At that time, I believed that my energy was better spent in trying to be successful than it was in dealing with my sexual identity. I wasn't able to focus on both issues at the same time and I didn't want anything getting in the way of my newly established purpose in life.

CHAPTER 9

Doctoral Degree

It Was the Best of Times, it Was the Worst of Times

With a great deal of apprehension, I started classes for my doctoral degree at the Michigan School of Professional Psychology in September 2004. About a month before the program began, I moved into another apartment near the school, which helped to reinforce the feeling that I was starting a new phase of my life. However, I was very anxious about whether I could emotionally survive in a doctoral program. I had failed at student teaching, I had just been diagnosed with an autism spectrum disorder, and I still felt much younger than others my age. I feared I would be completely out of my league next to my fellow students. I had been told that most of them were older than I and had years of workplace experience in the mental health profession. I had only worked part-time jobs teaching tennis. I was afraid I wouldn't be able to keep pace with such bright and accomplished people who already had psychology backgrounds and would be so much more mature than I. But, as I would soon discover, my classmates' maturity would end up benefitting me.

On the first day of class, I met the people with whom I would be spending the next four years, and most were already practicing psychotherapists. We went around in a circle and introduced ourselves. Everyone was so open and honest. Even though my heart felt as if it was beating out of my chest, when it came to my turn, I decided to disclose my Asperger's diagnosis. Immediately I felt an outpouring of support, as if my classmates were rooting for me to succeed in the program. I had never felt this kind of acceptance in any other setting before.

Sitting across from me in the circle was a friendly woman who was a few years older than I. Her name was Katie. When she introduced herself, she mentioned that she counseled parents of children with autism. She had also worked at the University of Michigan and started her own autism consulting practice. I was extremely impressed with her credentials, but more than that, I was delighted to learn that one of my classmates really understood autism and Asperger's. Meeting her at this point in my life seemed very serendipitous.

Katie and I became great friends right away. Her warmth, intelligence, and sense of humor made it easy for me to be around her. She never took herself too seriously, which was good because I took myself far too seriously. She was also quite feisty and spoke her mind, which I respected because I had trouble standing up for myself. Katie's academic and clinical knowledge of autism and Asperger's helped her to understand me and made it easy for me to trust her as a real friend. She was the first person, other than my parents, who ever got me! After a while, Katie felt like the big sister I never had.

She also helped me emotionally survive what proved to be a difficult program. Classes were extremely challenging for me in that they involved a lot of personal disclosure, group participation, experiential exercises, and role-playing. These types of interpersonal activities took me way out of my comfort zone. I had always preferred lecture classes where I could anonymously sit in the back of the room, go unnoticed, and not have to interact with anyone else. Katie was aware of the discomfort these activities created and gave me a stress ball to help me relax. Sometimes when I was stimming—unconsciously jiggling my leg in order to release nervous energy—she would gently tap me on the leg to make me aware of what I was doing. She also encouraged me to take breaks whenever I needed to. During these breaks, I would go to the school atrium and spend some time alone as a way of rejuvenating myself. In spite of the many difficulties I would encounter throughout the doctoral program, I always had a good friend sitting next to me who understood how I felt.

During my first year in the program, my dad and I had an idea. With my newfound understanding of Asperger's syndrome, we wanted to make a video documentary about my life and diagnosis. The goal of the video would be to show what having Asperger's was like and how it affected an individual with this condition and his or her family. Another objective was to educate teachers, mental health professionals, family members, and others who work with people with Asperger's, and help them to better understand this disorder.

My dad, who had previously produced documentaries for public television, was excited about this project. We decided to interview some of the people who were involved in my growth and development, including my speech therapist, my special education preschool teacher, a babysitter I had for many years, and my first tennis coach. They helped describe and explain some of the characteristics and traits of Asperger's and different aspects of my development. Dr Sheldrake, the neuropsychologist who diagnosed me, agreed to participate in the video as an expert on Asperger's who could discuss the broader and more clinical issues of being on the spectrum.

We also utilized home movies to bring my story to life through video clips beginning with when I was a toddler, jumping and flapping my arms right up to my appearance on *The Price Is Right*. Dad and I were quite proud of this DVD and we pitched it to the Gray Center, a wonderful organization in Grand Rapids that serves autistic individuals and their families. After they had viewed the DVD, my dad and I drove to Grand Rapids to meet with the two organizers of the Gray Center. They were very interested in distributing it. We were thrilled. This achievement was my entrance into the autism and Asperger's community.

Around this same time, my dad and I attended our first national autism conference in Nashville, Tennessee. Going to this conference was one of the most eye-opening experiences of my life. Many of the presenters were individuals like me who were on the autism spectrum. The three-day conference truly inspired me. I had never seen so many courageous people talk about themselves with such intelligence, humor, honesty, and dignity. And the best part was that I could identify with them.

Up until that conference, I hadn't realized that an autistic culture even existed. Moreover, some of the speakers embraced a point of view known as neurodiversity, which sees differences in neurological development not as handicaps or disabilities but rather as variances in human behavior. The neurodiversity movement seeks to honor autistic people just as they are, without trying to change or cure them. The concept that autism was a gift, not a deficit, was a completely novel approach that I had never even considered before. But it seemed true. Having Asperger's was now enabling me to make a difference in a positive way.

Shortly thereafter, Katie helped me to secure my first speaking engagement. I spoke at a conference called Choices in Autism, which was sponsored by an organization that ran a school and a clinic for autistic children. I was the last speaker of the day and was allotted thirty minutes for my presentation. My topic was simply my life as a person with Asperger's. Even though I had made a DVD about my life story, I really didn't consider myself to be an interesting person. I wasn't sure that an audience would want to sit there for thirty minutes and listen to me talk about myself. I was terrified to walk on stage but I remembered the success I felt at my Bar Mitzvah and hoped something similar would happen. Katie could see I was freaking out so she and I took a walk in the parking lot right before my talk, which helped to calm me down. When it was my turn to take the stage, I literally read from my script. It wasn't a particularly dynamic presentation but I got through it. Katie was there not only to support me, but also to press the button for each slide in my PowerPoint presentation. After I finished speaking, the reaction I got overwhelmed me. The audience applauded enthusiastically. Parents came up and told me what an inspiration I was and that they hoped someday their kids would turn out like me. I couldn't believe it. Me? An inspiration?

People asked me how, as someone with Asperger's, I could deal with all the anxiety typically involved in getting up and speaking in front of an audience. They didn't understand that, for me, delivering a PowerPoint presentation was a totally scripted experience. I knew that I just needed to follow along step by step as to what came next and I wouldn't have to deal with any uncertainty. Having a spontaneous conversation with just one other person was infinitely scarier because I could never predict what the other person might say and how I should react.

A couple of months later, I contacted the local library and asked if they might be interested in a free public showing of my DVD. They were extremely interested and placed an advertisement in the local paper announcing my presentation. The organizers set up twenty-five chairs expecting a small crowd, as was the usual case for guest speakers at this library. Nearly two hundred people showed up. The organizers of the event and I were shocked that so many people came. The audience consisted of children and adolescents on the spectrum, their parents and extended families, as well as teachers and therapists who worked with them. Who knew this would be such a hot topic?

After the DVD was shown, I spoke for about ten or fifteen minutes and then took questions from the audience. As if my life had direct relevance to their children's lives, parents asked me personal questions: "Did your parents always have to nag you to do your homework?" "Did you have any friends in middle school?" Some people actually sought my advice on issues: "My kid always comes home from school in a bad mood and I can't get him to talk. What should I do?" My inclination was to say, "Why are you asking me? I'm not Dr Spock." Instead I gave the best answers I could and surprisingly, they came out all right. Receiving all this attention, respect, and even being viewed as an expert that night was a completely new experience that overwhelmed and excited me.

Soon after this talk, I began to receive other invitations from local groups and organizations asking me to speak about Asperger's. With each experience, I found myself improving in my delivery and speaking style, and I didn't have to rely so closely on a script. Parents continued to respond positively to me as if I were a role model. But talking about my life over and over again seemed narcissistic to me. I wanted to start using my doctoral studies to do research and broaden my area of expertise to topics that had negatively affected me as an effort to help others struggling with similar issues. So I approached the Gray Center again, this time with the idea of making a DVD about bullying prevention. The Gray Center told me they did not have the budget to produce another DVD but referred me to Jessica Kingsley Publishers (JKP). I submitted a proposal to JKP and they agreed to distribute the bullying DVD. In making the DVD, I wove together my firsthand experience as a victim of bullying with available research on both Asperger's and bullying. Because I had been bullied severely as a child, this subject was and is extremely personal to me. In my mind, if I could prevent one person from experiencing the torment I endured throughout public school, I would feel like a success.

After the bullying DVD was distributed, I received many invitations to speak about bullying prevention at various schools, organizations, and conferences. I also gave some interviews on radio and television. Because of the success of this DVD, JKP asked me if I would be interested in writing a book proposal on the same subject. I agreed and subsequently wrote a book about bullying prevention and Asperger's syndrome. This book sold very well and elicited many more speaking engagements all over the country. I could hardly believe I had written a book, produced two DVDs, and given numerous speeches, all while I was in a doctoral program. My intellect and creativity were flourishing, but I was beginning to feel stretched thin.

Two years earlier I had stopped seeing Dr Green. After I got my diagnosis, I left Dr Green and switched to Dr Sheldrake because he was an expert in Asperger's syndrome and had just diagnosed me. For a while, I liked working with someone who knew so much about Asperger's. I would come home glowing from our sessions because Dr Sheldrake understood certain aspects about me that no one ever had before. For example, he could connect my social deficits to having Asperger's in a way that other therapists could not. He had a neurological perspective as opposed to a strictly psychological perspective on many of my problems. However, when I brought up the issue of my sexual identity, Dr Sheldrake seemed uncomfortable in dealing with this issue. So I decided to take a break from therapy. I was succeeding in graduate school and making a name for myself in the Asperger's and autism community. For the first time, things were going well in my life. Maybe I didn't even need to see a therapist. It felt as if I had been seeing therapists all my life. I was sick of seeing therapists. So I took a two-year hiatus from therapy.

In that time, I became even busier with school and my career. I gave speeches in Massachusetts, Pennsylvania, Virginia, Florida, Texas, Maine, New York, Minnesota, Kentucky, Indiana, and Hawaii. I spoke at the National Jewish Book Fair along with such notable authors as Alan Dershowitz and Jeffrey Toobin. I was also asked to write a bi-monthly column for the *Autism Asperger's Digest*, a magazine with worldwide distribution. During these years, I took on more than I could handle, but I couldn't say no to anyone who asked me to give a presentation, even if they weren't able to pay me a fee. Katie continually expressed concern about my being too overworked with my studies and all my other pursuits. She saw all the pressure I was under and the toll it was taking on me in terms of anxiety and depression.

I was also becoming increasingly uncomfortable within my own skin. For example, parents of children with Asperger's often asked me at conferences: "Do you date?" or "Do you plan on getting married?" I didn't know what to say because these questions inadvertently struck an extremely raw nerve within in me. This was the only subject that I couldn't respond to comfortably. Usually, I'd give a general answer like, "I'm open to anything," but the truth was I was still terrified of being homosexual.

This fear increased to the point where I even confided in Katie that I thought I might be "G...A...Y." She had the same reaction as Dr Green had years earlier when I couldn't even say the word. She said she loved me whether I was gay or not, but I was afraid if other people knew, I might not get invited to speak anymore and I would be ostracized by the autism community. These were unfounded beliefs that had no merit in reality, but at the time I believed they were true. I didn't want to jeopardize my success in the Asperger's world, and the anxiety and stress that these fears were generating was building to a dangerous crescendo.

Externally, I was succeeding beyond my wildest expectations, but internally I was an emotional wreck. My coping strategies were nonexistent. I was isolating myself more than ever, binge eating, not exercising, and had put on thirty pounds in just a few months.

My graduate studies and my new career were creating an even deeper divide between my intellectual growth and my social, emotional, and sexual development. Even though I was doing very adult things, inside it was a different story. I still felt like a much younger person trying to play catch up. For example, I could travel anywhere in the country and give an articulate speech, but I wouldn't have dinner with the organizer of the event because of my extreme social discomfort. I could write the first draft of a book in five or six months, but I still had made no friends, other than Katie. And sexually, I was a pre-adolescent frozen in time, a situation that was becoming more and more painful to me. This ever-widening gap between my intellectual and social/sexual development was creating a sense of desperation and futility, which is why I finally decided to return to Dr Green.

Since my diagnosis, my parents were concerned that Dr Green didn't have sufficient knowledge about Asperger's to treat me because he primarily dealt with sexual issues. They felt it was extremely important that the therapist I now work with have a solid understanding of Asperger's in order to be effective. Although Dr Sheldrake had that understanding, he lacked expertise in sexuality, which I also needed. My parents tried to find a therapist who had expertise in both areas, but none existed. So my parents met with Dr Green and he told them that he felt confident treating me even though he acknowledged his lack of expertise in Asperger's.

When I next saw Dr Green, I was eager to bring him up-to-date on the last two years of my life. I proudly filled him in all my achievements, but let him know that they came at a very high price. I also told him that all the fears I had previously discussed with him (being gay, my parents predeceasing me, being unemployable) were still there and had become even more intense and debilitating.

Along with these fears, I told him I felt extremely depressed that all my attempts to deal with my sexual identity had been unsuccessful. In response, Dr Green suggested that I use adult pornography magazines as a way to assess my sexual interests. He told me this type of exploration would be less stressful for me because I wouldn't have to confront my fears of interacting with others. Following his suggestion, I went to a rather seedy part of town, found an adult bookstore, and bought some sexually explicit adult heterosexual and homosexual magazines. After looking at the various pictures in these magazines, I reluctantly started to admit to myself that I preferred the homosexual images.

Like many people with Asperger's who have little social contact, my computer was my major link to the outside world. I relied heavily on it to gather research for my studies, to obtain information about my special interests, and as a way to connect with others. For example, I would spend hours every day on the internet finding jazz music and then I would post all my recommendations on Facebook.

At the time, it seemed like a natural progression for me to go from looking at pornographic magazines to viewing the same type of material on the computer. Using the computer was certainly a more comfortable and safer way to explore my sexuality than dating, traveling to Nevada, or going to adult bookstores.

As I began looking at images of adult males on the computer, I was surprised at how easy this material was to access and that it was free of charge. I soon discovered that other links to more sexually explicit websites would spontaneously pop up unbidden in my view. This process eventually led me to images of minors. I was curious. Looking at these images seemed like another way to explore my sexuality because a part of me felt as if I was the same age as the pictures I was looking at. Although I felt a sense of shame when I viewed these images, I did not do so as an adult wanting to have physical contact with them. The images I viewed did not involve violence of any kind or adults shown with children. In fact, the thought of an adult engaging in sexual activity with a minor was and is extremely repulsive to me.

I told Dr Green that I had looked at pornography on my computer, both of adult and pre-adolescent males. He said viewing adult pornography could be therapeutic but that it was wrong to look at images of minors. At the time I didn't understand that downloading free images on my computer in the privacy of my residence could lead to the severe legal consequences I later experienced.

I also didn't understand at the time that the children in the images had been victimized in the process of creating those images. I honestly had no idea that I was causing harm to anyone. It is very embarrassing to admit that I needed to have this information spelled out for me, as I wasn't able to make that connection on my own. After my arrest, Dr Green spent considerable time explaining the issue of victim awareness to me. I was horrified to learn that these minors had been mistreated and that I had not been able to see that. I know deep in my heart that if I had been aware that those children had been abused, I would have never looked at those images again.

In his chapter, Dr Tony Attwood discusses the concept of impaired Theory of Mind, an inability to perceive what others are thinking and feeling—in other words, the ability to put oneself in someone else's shoes. Dr Green, in his report to the prosecutors, acknowledged my lack of awareness that these children were victims: "It is highly unlikely Nick fully appreciated the magnitude of his offense. It is my strong opinion that Nick failed to make the association between viewing child pornography and the harm done to child victims of child pornography."

I continued to focus on many other problems in therapy besides my sexuality. I was extremely busy with school and my speaking career, which helped to further obfuscate my sexual issues. My sexuality wasn't just on the back burner. It wasn't on any burner at all in terms of therapy. I was in constant crisis trying to keep up with the demands of my life, which drew Dr Green's attention away from my sexual issues.

I was now nearing the end of my doctoral degree and working hard on my dissertation. I was also writing another book for JKP and had joined the board of directors of two autism organizations. At school, I was starting a new internship working at a human service agency that focused on autism. There was no doubt that I was burning the candle at both ends and, at times, I felt like a human pressure cooker that was ready to explode.

In spite of all this turmoil, I somehow managed to complete my coursework, finish my dissertation, and graduate with my doctoral degree in psychology. Now I faced a new challenge. How was I going to use my doctoral degree to gain employment? My best friend, Katie, was moving out of state because her husband received a job transfer. She was starting a new life without me so I had to do the same. Because I didn't seek licensure, there weren't a lot of options. I could continue to give speeches and write books, but self-employment didn't provide financial security or health insurance. I wanted to become financially independent. Since my diagnosis, I was aware that so many intelligent and capable people with Asperger's are either unemployed or underemployed and I didn't want to fall into either category.

Around this time my mom heard about a new high school that was opening for students with Asperger's syndrome about an hour away from where I lived. She suggested I make contact with the headmaster to see if they might need a consultant. I initially resisted the idea because of my difficulties with prior work experience.

I told Dr Green about this potential opportunity and asked him for his thoughts. He encouraged me to contact the school, emphasizing that I shouldn't let fear of failure stop me from taking on new experiences. So with Dr Green's blessing, I made an appointment to meet with the headmaster.

This was my first real job interview. I was terrified but was soon put at ease when I met the headmaster. I was surprised he knew so little about Asperger's. After recently learning that his grandson had the condition, he decided to start this school. He had been a public school teacher for forty years but this venture was his first role as the head of a private institution. I told him about my background and he seemed impressed with all my writings, presentations, and life experience with Asperger's. He told me to go home and write my own job description and email it to him. I sent him a number of ways I thought I could assist him and his teachers in meeting the needs of his students. A month later, he offered me a job.

My primary role at the school was helping the teachers and headmaster learn as much as possible about Asperger's so that they could better serve the students. The teachers were highly qualified in the subjects they taught but did not have any background in special education. I threw myself into the job, creating an in-service consultancy for teachers before classes began. Once school started, I consulted with the teachers about how they could make their subject matter clearer to the students. I also began to organize a major conference on Asperger's and booked several well-known speakers to come to the school. I felt excited about trying to create the kind of educational environment that I didn't receive when I went through public school. I was finally accomplishing my goal in life: I was making a difference.

Only a month after I started this new job, I was arrested by the FBI. That day everything in my life came to a complete halt. I had no idea how tortuous every day of the next two-and-a-half years would become for my parents and for me as we waited in a kind of hellish limbo for the criminal justice system to decide my fate.

CHAPTER 10

United States of America v. Nicolas Dubin

The FBI raid on my apartment took place on the morning of October 6, 2010. Shortly after the agents left, my dad called an attorney. Later that day, my dad received a call from an assistant United States attorney formally informing him that my arraignment would be the very next day. My dad now had the formidable task of trying to explain to me what was going to happen the following day. He used very simple language, knowing I didn't even have the basic legal understanding of what the word "arraignment" meant. He told me I would be appearing before a magistrate on a complaint that had been filed against me by the United States government. I asked very few questions. I was afraid to hear the answers and was still shaken from the FBI raid earlier that day. That night I didn't sleep at all.

Having no clue what was in store for me, the next day my dad accompanied me to the Theodore Levin United States Courthouse in downtown Detroit. A federal courthouse is an extremely imposing place. There is a heavy presence of US Marshals everywhere. I had to go through security, but it felt a lot more intimidating than going through security at an airport. I also saw a number of prisoners walking around in orange jumpsuits as they were being processed and getting ready to be sent to jail. Was I about to become one of them? The entire situation was frightening and Kafkaesque.

The first event of that day was an interview with a pretrial services officer. My dad wanted to be there to support me. He was denied access. The pretrial officer asked me about my finances, whether I was suicidal, where I lived, and a lot of other questions that would help the magistrate determine what kind of bond I would have that would permit me to be released from custody. Bond? Custody? Release? Were these words really being applied to me?

There was a two-hour break between the interview and my court appearance, and my dad and I were allowed to step outside the courthouse. I was extremely nervous and was pacing back and forth. Originally, I was to be placed in a holding cell during this time, but thankfully my lawyer was able to find a way to avoid that. I couldn't believe what was happening to me. Just a day ago, I was a consultant at a high school for individuals with Asperger's syndrome and a national speaker on autism, but in a couple of hours, I would be walking into a federal courtroom as an accused criminal. I didn't know who I was any more and had never been so terrified in my life.

Inside the courtroom, I recognized one of the FBI agents who had interrogated me at my apartment the day before. He and one of the assistant US attorneys who were prosecuting my case were present, along with a packed courtroom of spectators, including accused criminals, their lawyers, and members of the media. It was horrifying to think my case would ever be on the news, but I didn't have time to dwell on that possibility. My most immediate concern was to make it through the arraignment in one piece. My dad sat beside me in the gallery as we waited for my case to be called. He tried to be stoic, but I could tell by his grim expression he was almost as scared as I was. A number of cases were called before mine and the magistrate informed each of these defendants how long their prison sentences might be if they were found guilty of the charges brought against them. Some defendants were immediately taken into custody while others were released on bond. Watching these proceedings made my whole body quake with fear.

Finally, the court clerk called my case: "United States of America versus Nicolas Dubin." My heart was pounding so loud I thought it would come out of my chest. My lawyer stood beside me as the magistrate conducted the arraignment and explained the conditions I would have to follow to stay out of jail before my trial. She also told me I was going to have to wear a tether. A tether? What's a tether? I asked myself. I found out soon enough. As I turned from the podium to walk back down the aisle of the gallery, it felt as if everyone sitting there was giving me cold, hard stares. Whether those stares were real or imagined, it almost didn't matter. I felt an overwhelming sense of shame.

After the arraignment, I had to go to the scariest area of the courthouse: the lockup unit. This area is like a small jail where prisoners wait in holding cells. I will never forget the image of grown men sitting alone in their individual cells with video monitors surveying their every movement. The lockup unit is where I had my mugshot and fingerprints taken. Two more surreal events that I could not believe were actually happening to me.

From there, I was ordered back to pretrial services, where I met a different pretrial services officer who would be supervising me while I was on release. For six months, I was to report to him twice a month and if I obeyed the conditions during that time, it would go down to once a month. As it turned out I was on release for a total of thirty-one months. This pretrial officer was cold and stern and showed no sign of emotion. The thought of meeting with this man one time, let alone twice a month, was a horrifying prospect.

"What I'm about to put on your ankle is a tether," he said. "This tether will monitor your movements. You will not leave your house before 8:00 a.m. in the morning and you must be home by 8:00 p.m. every night. This is a court order. Do you understand, Mr Dubin?"

"Yes Sir," I said, my voice barely audible.

"You will not so much as step foot outside your door after 8:00 p.m. And when I say a foot, I mean not even on your front porch. If you do, we will know about it. US Marshals will come and take you away to jail. Do I make myself clear?"

"Yes Officer," I said.

The FBI raid and my appearance in court the next day would have been extremely stressful situations for anyone to go through, but for someone with Asperger's, they were unimaginably frightening. People on the autism spectrum have great difficulty with change, especially sudden change, because there is no time to prepare for what is going to happen. The number of sudden transitions, unexpected situations, unanswered questions, and the dramatic, overnight change in my life made these two events unspeakably difficult for me. But, as I was soon to find out, this was only the beginning of my nightmare.

The day after my court appearance, my parents and I met with my lawyer, Ken Mogill, at his office. He had been a practicing criminal defense attorney for over forty years. Just being in his presence was comforting after being arraigned and processed the day before. One thing he said during that meeting that gave me hope was, "I don't like to lose, Nick. By my very nature, I am a fighter." Although his comment gave me hope, it also sounded cavalier and a bit trivializing. I immediately thought: *What is this? A game?* Of course, I now have a much fuller appreciation and understanding of what he meant.

During that meeting he took a life history and the facts of my case began to emerge. Even though Ken is a kind and thoughtful person, I was still mortified that I had to divulge to him that I had virtually no sexual experience and an extremely limited social life that went all the way back to my toddler years. My parents also gave Ken many reports written by medical, mental health, and educational professionals that documented my development over the years. In the early childhood reports, neurological problems had become apparent, such as jumping up and down, flapping my arms, and isolating myself from other children. He thought these reports were important because they showed a history of neurological issues that began very early in my life.

Ken felt strongly that it would be best not to have my case placed on the court's trial docket. He believed the stresses and strains of a trial would be too difficult for my family and me, and thought we might get a better result by trying to negotiate a plea agreement that would divert me from the criminal justice system into a program of supervision. When a case is not on the trial docket, there are no time requirements to be met so consequently there can be a lot of very long delays.

Ten days after my arraignment a shocking new development occurred. There was a news story about my case on a local television station. I found out about it when a board member of an Asperger's organization with whom I had served called to tell me he had seen the story on the internet that day. I was mortified that this man, who I greatly respected and who lived in another state, had read this story on the internet. He was very supportive of me but after the story came out, the board decided to let me go.

I still haven't read this news story and don't ever plan to, but I know that it spread very quickly throughout the Asperger's cyberspace community. Some people wrote me encouraging letters of support while I heard others vilified me on the internet. From what I was told, the story presented inaccurate and very damaging information. I was horrified to think that people with whom I had professional and personal contact had now learned what had happened. I was devastated and wanted to end my life. I knew that many of these people now viewed me as a predator and a pedophile, and there was nothing I could do about it. It was painful to know that what was being said about me was untrue and yet I was powerless to do anything about it.

After the story appeared on the internet, I literally hid in my house. I would only go out if I absolutely had to and would not leave if there were even one neighbor outside. I wore a cap, pulled down low over my face, and sunglasses so no one would recognize me. My shame was so great that I also stopped seeing family members, other than my parents, and became completely isolated.

Overnight, I had lost my reputation and everything else I had worked so hard for, including my apartment. I had been living on my own for nine years and enjoyed my privacy. But after the FBI raid, I couldn't imagine ever living in the same place where that traumatic event had occurred, and so I moved back home with my parents the day of my arrest. I felt like the protagonist in a Shakespearean tragedy, who loses everything because of a tragic flaw of which he is not aware until it is too late.

A week after the arraignment, I had to have an individual intake interview for the sex offender group that I was ordered to attend. I was incredibly anxious about it. For someone with Asperger's, being in any kind of a group creates great apprehension and anxiety, and I instinctively knew that being in a group of sex offenders was neither something I needed nor could handle. What I needed was a trusting, safe environment where I would feel supported and I could deal with the tragic mistakes I had made and learn from them. But this group and its leader were anything but supportive.

My dad and I were sitting in the waiting room when the group leader came out to get me. My dad was wearing a suit.

"Are you his lawyer?" the group leader asked hostilely, as we were walking back to his office.

"I'm a lawyer but I'm also his father," my dad answered politely. "I'm not his lawyer for this case."

"I don't meet with lawyers. Period! You can have a seat back in the waiting room."

"Wait a minute," my dad said. "My son has a disability called Asperger's syndrome. This is very traumatic for him and I just want to be here to support him."

"Sir, if you're not going to cooperate, I can call his pretrial services officer and we can arrange for your son to be transported to jail. Now, what's your pleasure?" With that kind of a threat, my dad had no choice but to acquiesce.

For the next hour-and-a-half, the group leader and I were alone in his office. He told me that the more I participated in the group, the better his reports would be to my pretrial services officer, which would influence the kind of sentence I would get. I later learned from my lawyer, and other group members who spoke to me privately, that anything you say in the group is not confidential and can be used against you in court. Participation was encouraged, but everyone in the group knew that they couldn't be "too open," just open enough to appear cooperative.

The first session was a week after the intake interview. The group leader came in with a Big Mac in his hand and was eating it as he asked us to go around the room and introduce ourselves. We had to say our names and what we were accused of doing. The guy sitting next to me said that in a few days he would be leaving the group because he was being sentenced to fourteen years in a federal penitentiary for crimes related to child pornography. Fourteen years! It was another jaw dropping moment for me. When I came home that night I was hysterical for hours. At another session, a participant told me privately that he was acting as a "snitch" or informant in a drug bust in an effort to work out a plea bargain with the government. I might have heard the terms informant and plea bargain before, but I didn't know what they meant. This was way too much information for me to deal with all at once. I was on emotional overload.

I attended several group sessions and had a severe meltdown after each one. Hearing about the possibility of going to prison terrified me. I would come home consumed with panic and started telling my parents I wanted to die. My parents became very concerned that I could have a complete breakdown and might need to be hospitalized. Ken called my pretrial services officer and tried to explain my disability and how negatively this group was impacting me. His call fell on deaf ears. Dr Green wrote a letter to that same effect to the officer. Again, he said no. Ken then had a conference call with the group leader and my pretrial services officer, referencing the letter from Dr Green and begging them for understanding. Once again, they both said no. Finally, Ken made a motion to the court and submitted a report, written by an expert in Asperger's, that explained why a group setting affected me so negatively. This motion went uncontested by the prosecution for a month, so I was permitted to leave the group and instead attend private therapy twice a week, which my parents paid for.

During my extensive post-arrest therapy I came to realize the seriousness of my actions. Before the arrest, I was simply not aware that I was participating in a culture of abuse. I truly did not understand that the children in these pictures were victims. I was mortified that I wasn't aware of this before, but the sad truth is I wasn't. I know it is hard to comprehend that someone with a doctoral degree in psychology could have been so naive. I sincerely regret, and will always regret for the rest of my life, that I had this blind spot.

The next step was to find a forensic psychologist who specialized in autism spectrum disorders and who could evaluate me in relation to the charges that had been brought against me. Finding a forensic psychologist who had expertise in both Asperger's and sexuality was impossible. Generally, an expert in sexuality will not know much about autism and vice versa.

After two months of searching, we were finally referred to Dr Andrew Maltz, a psychologist with a specialty in autism spectrum disorders. Between Dr Maltz and Dr Green, we had the issues of autism and sexuality both covered.

The first meeting with Dr Maltz consisted of him interviewing my parents and me for ninety minutes. At the end of that meeting, I told Dr Maltz how terrified I was of being sent to prison and that I couldn't imagine surviving the experience. I wanted some kind of reassurance that this would never be the case, but he would only say he didn't know me well enough to be able to make any kind of determinations yet. In other words, he wasn't going to be on my side simply because he was hired by my lawyer. He told me he was going to base his opinions on my life history, his review and corroboration of my Asperger's diagnosis, and the results of several psychological tests he would be giving to me.

In the second session Dr Maltz interviewed me alone for two hours. He tried to get a sense of what motivated me to view child pornography. As uncomfortable and embarrassing as this was, I knew I had to be totally honest with him. I told him that when I engaged in this behavior, I imagined myself being the age I was in middle school and the minors in these images as the kids who I wanted to be my friends. I had not just come up with this explanation, but had uncovered this insight over the past few months in my therapy with Dr Green. I also told Dr Maltz how ashamed I was of my behavior and that I would never harm a child.

During the third session he gave me a full battery of psychological tests, including the Vineland Adaptive Behavior Scales, which give age equivalencies that show how well one adapts to the basic areas of life, such as social interaction, hygiene, and skills of independent living. In other words, this test measures one's "emotional" or "psychosocial age" as opposed to how someone would score on an IQ test, where large gaps exist for those on the spectrum. To my dismay, other than my intellect, the Vineland showed I had the age equivalent of a pre-adolescent in many areas of my life. Given that is the age I have felt most of my life, I shouldn't have been so surprised, but I was still shocked to see a test confirm that feeling. Dr Maltz independently asked my parents the same questions from the Vineland about me, and their answers were nearly identical to mine.

In addition, he gave me the Minnesota Multiphasic Psychological Inventory (MMPI) that asks questions in a way that makes it impossible for someone to lie and not be detected. The MMPI assesses one's personality profile, but Dr Maltz's main objective was to find out whether I had any psychopathic tendencies. The results showed I did not. After the interviews and testing, Dr Maltz reviewed all the reports from my early childhood culminating with my Asperger's diagnosis at age twenty-seven. He also talked extensively with Dr Green about my treatment, as well as to my psychiatrist who prescribed antidepressants and anti-anxiety medication for me. After three meetings with Dr Maltz, he gave no indication what he would say in his report.

Meanwhile, Ken decided to contact a former US attorney and chief of the criminal division of the office that was now prosecuting me. Ken approached him to see if he would have any interest in representing me as co-counsel. Since leaving the prosecutor's office, he had been often asked to be a defense lawyer, but had declined every time, because as Ken explained he still was a prosecutor at heart. Ken thought he would be able to help my defense by viewing my case from a prosecutor's perspective. Ken went over the unique circumstances of my case and he agreed to meet me but without any obligation to join the defense. I was not prepared for how direct and confrontational he would be. He looked me right in the eye and said in a stern tone that when he was a prosecutor in the US attorney's office, he always prosecuted the crime I had been charged with to the fullest extent of the law. He said he understood I wanted him to represent me but that first, I needed to convince him why he should.

I was so intimidated by him that I honestly don't remember the rest of the conversation, but two things were very clear from this meeting. First, for him to agree to represent me, he had to be convinced beyond a shadow of a doubt that I was not a threat to children. After a thirty-year career as a federal prosecutor, he was not about to represent someone against his former office who he felt was a danger to society. Second, he needed to believe there was a legitimate reason as to why I should not be criminally prosecuted for this crime. At the end of our meeting, he said that he was glad to meet me and needed time to think about whether he wanted to represent me. A week later, he contacted Ken and said, after much thought, he had decided to join him as co-counsel. He said he believed I had told him the truth and that, although he didn't know enough yet about Asperger's, this stood out to him as a unique and compelling case.

At the same time, my dad contacted a highly respected and leading expert in Asperger's, Dr Fred Volkmar, head of the Child Study Center at Yale University, who agreed to evaluate me as well. Ken motioned the court for permission for me to travel to New Haven, Connecticut for this evaluation. During the entire trip, I had to wear a GPS device, which was bigger and a lot more cumbersome than the tether. Going through security at the airport made me feel extremely self-conscious, because I had to be pulled aside by the Transport Security Administration, who knew because I was wearing a GPS device that I was a criminal of some kind. I was told the device had to be charged every twelve hours, but after only three, it started buzzing in the middle of the flight. I couldn't wait to get to the hotel and recharge it so it would stop. At night, I slept with the GPS unit plugged into the wall outlet so it wouldn't start buzzing in the middle of the night.

The next day I met with Dr Volkmar, who had received and read all of the previous reports and records. I spent one-and-a-half hours with him and basically told him the same things I had told Dr Maltz. Then my dad and I flew back to Detroit and traded in the GPS unit for the good old tether. I never thought I would be happy to be wearing that tether again.

Dr Maltz and Dr Volkmar both wrote positive reports on my behalf. Dr Maltz's report was extremely detailed and covered almost every area of my life. He concluded that I had an autism spectrum disorder, that he did not view me as a risk for being a predator, and that psychosocially and psychosexually I was the age equivalent of a pre-adolescent. Although I was humiliated and even angered by this last conclusion, I couldn't deny the truth of his findings.

Five months after the arraignment, my lawyers submitted the reports of Drs Green, Maltz, and Volkmar to the prosecutors. Based on these reports, they asserted that justice would best be served if I were to receive pretrial diversion instead of a prison sentence or probation. Unlike probation where one is convicted as a lifelong felon and has to register as a sex offender, diversion provides a second chance by permitting someone to complete a period of supervision (usually 18 months) while complying with a set of prescribed conditions. If rehabilitation occurs during that time, the criminal charges are dropped, thereby avoiding a lifelong felony conviction and the stigma and restrictions of being a sex offender. Diversion is given to those who are not assumed to be criminal types, have no history of drug addiction, and are believed to have the potential to be rehabilitated. Both my lawyers, as well as all three experts, were convinced I was a good candidate for diversion, which was their conclusion in their submission to the prosecutors.

After waiting three months for a response to this submission, we finally heard from the prosecutors, and it was not good news. They would not consider diversion, but the reports had convinced them that I was not a danger to children and that autism had played a role in my culpability. Therefore, the prosecutors decided not to seek prison, which was a tremendous relief for me. I would be spared being separated from my parents on whom I was so dependent, and I would not be placed in an environment that I did not think I could survive even for a day.

Although having prison taken off the table was a major relief, the prosecution was still insisting on a conviction, which meant being a lifelong felon and a registered sex offender. My lawyers were not satisfied with this offer. After speaking to one of the prosecutors, Ken felt that, in spite of the three experts' comprehensive reports, the prosecution didn't understand the difference between Asperger's and mental illness. In an effort to further educate them, Ken asked

Dr Maltz and Dr Green to each write a supplemental report, clarifying this distinction. These reports were then submitted to the prosecutors, who said they would be open to reading them.

Our family waited for several agonizing months for the prosecutors to respond to these supplementary reports. It was pure torture waiting every day for the phone to ring or an email to arrive with some news. For someone on the spectrum, dealing with uncertainty creates tremendous anxiety, but when that uncertainty goes on for months, and the rest of your life is at stake, it is truly unbearable. Sadly, when the answer finally came, the prosecution had still not changed their position. They would not agree to diversion and would only accept a felony conviction and sex offender registration.

Again, my lawyers did not want to accept this offer. The case had been going on now for almost a year and they felt very strongly that diversion was the correct resolution for my case. Ken asked the prosecutors if they had used an expert of their own to review our reports. They said they had not. Ken then requested that they choose a qualified government expert, with a background in Asperger's, to review these reports and then examine me. They believed that if the prosecutors' own expert corroborated our experts' conclusions, they would have no choice but to act in good faith and offer diversion. This strategy showed me that my lawyers truly believed in my case and the legitimacy of our experts' opinions. We breathed a sigh of relief when the prosecutors agreed to hold off on filing the indictment and said they would consider Ken's request.

A month later, the prosecutors said they had chosen their own government expert to examine me. This expert was an FBI neuropsychologist in Washington DC who was also the head of the Victim Assistance Program, which includes victims of child pornography. In addition, he had postgraduate training in autism spectrum disorders from Johns Hopkins University. Now my choice was either to take the previously offered plea or to travel to the J. Edgar Hoover Building FBI headquarters in Washington DC and go through another extensive interview with this expert.

Terrified by either choice, I sought input from the people I trusted most: my lawyers, my parents, Dr Green, my friend Katie, who had been recently diagnosed with breast cancer, and Julia, our family counselor. Everyone thought I should do it. My lawyers told me the prosecutors had assured them that after this evaluation, they would need nothing more to come to a decision. My dad had some concern about the objectivity of an FBI employee, who protects children in pornography cases, evaluating me. Ken said his concern was real, but that he sensed a new openness in the prosecutors not closing the door and having me be evaluated by a government expert. He also said he had complete confidence in our experts, whose reports would be made available to this FBI psychologist.

I waited a month before the appointment was scheduled in Washington DC. The anticipatory anxiety I felt was excruciating. Ken said there was no way to prepare me for this examination, other than to be myself and to be completely honest. Everything seemed to be riding on this evaluation, so it felt as if I was living in a pressure cooker. I couldn't put my worries aside, even for one minute. On top of watching Katie's health deteriorate, I now had to get ready for what would be the most important meeting of my life.

The day before the appointment, my dad and I flew to Washington DC. The same curfew conditions I had at home applied to the night I spent in DC. After we got settled in our hotel, the first thing I wanted to do was to walk by the FBI building. I often prepared for giving a speech by visiting the venue beforehand. I found it helped calm my nerves to actually see an environment before I had to enter it. Of course, I couldn't go inside the building, but at least I wanted to observe it from the outside.

I told my dad that this interview was the scariest thing I'd ever had to do and bombarded him with questions. Would the fact that this psychologist worked for the FBI prejudice him against me from the start? Would I faint from just being in the J. Edgar Hoover Building that made the Federal Building in downtown Detroit look like a dollhouse? Would he interrogate me, in the same aggressive way the FBI agents did at my apartment, leaving me more vulnerable than ever?

The next morning, we arrived at the J. Edgar Hoover Building for our scheduled 10:00 a.m. appointment. I was a complete wreck and so was my father, who seemed shakier than I had ever seen him. Once inside the building we showed our identification to some guards and were led through two security checks. The FBI building was like a fortress and was so well guarded that even a mouse couldn't enter without having the proper authorization. It felt like a paramilitary building and, essentially, that's what it is. As visitors, my dad and I couldn't even use the bathroom without being personally escorted there while the guard waited outside the stall.

After waiting for a half an hour, the FBI neuropsychologist came to the lobby to greet us, walking at a fast-clipped and confident pace. He was tall and self-assured, and seemed as if he came right out of central casting. He escorted my dad and me through a maze of hallways and corridors that were dizzying and disorientating. Then, in a small interrogation room, he explained his role to me—that the prosecution had asked him to evaluate me and that anything I said could be used against me.

After he obtained my written consent, he proceeded to ask me questions for the next four-and-a-half hours. Nothing was off limits. The questions ranged from my Apgar score (a method used to assess the health of a newborn baby) at birth to my scholastic achievements, and finally to my motivation and state of mind when I viewed the images of minors on my computer. Even though many of his questions were extremely personal and, at times, humiliating, I took Ken's advice and answered all of them truthfully. He also performed a detailed risk assessment so that he could report back to the prosecutors whether I was a danger to children. After we were done with the evaluation, he gave me no indication as to what his findings and conclusions would be. He did tell my dad and me that he would write a report if the prosecutors requested one. It was a Friday and he said he would call the prosecutors on Monday to discuss my evaluation. As we left the FBI building, I was physically and emotionally drained.

My dad and I then took an airport van from Washington DC to Baltimore. We couldn't talk about what we had just experienced because there were other people sitting too close to us in the crowded van. I was very frustrated that I wasn't able to talk to my dad about what had just happened. At times, I would try to bring the subject up but he would just shush me. Because we hit rush-hour traffic, the ride to the airport took three hours instead of the forty-five to fifty minutes it should have taken and we barely made it to the plane. Again, because of the close proximity to others, we weren't able to discuss the events of the day on the plane. It would be another two-and-a-half hours before we were in our car back in Detroit. By that time my dad was so tired, he didn't have the energy to talk about our day, but that didn't stop me from asking him a million questions. Do you think today will help me? Could this exam have made things worse? Do you think I could get diversion now?

In retrospect, I can see where I was insensitive to my dad's needs and was only thinking about my own. But I was scared. My dad usually keeps his cool under pressure and provides me with a reassuring presence I badly need when I'm experiencing a stressful situation. However, the truth was my dad was as worried and exhausted as I was. It was scary to see my dad looking so vulnerable.

Two weeks had passed since our trip to Washington DC and there was no word from the prosecutor's office. My parents and I were very anxious. The first thing I said every morning when I woke up was, "Have we heard anything yet?" It was literally all I could think about. Because the FBI neuropsychologist had said he would contact the prosecutors that Monday, we thought we would have surely heard something by now. As the weeks went by, my mom and I became increasingly tense and pressured my dad to call Ken. We wanted him to contact the prosecutors to find out what was going on, but Ken felt it was too soon. I felt he didn't seem to understand that, for someone with Asperger's, the protracted waiting and uncertainty were torture. He told us it could take time for the prosecutors to receive the psychologist's report and then to evaluate it. He also said he didn't want to appear overanxious or show any sign of weakness. I wanted to say, "Forget all your strategies! I need some relief or I'm going to go crazy!"

Another couple of months went by and there was still no word from the prosecutors. I thought my lawyers would now be ready to contact them, but I was wrong. In spite of them knowing how anxious the waiting was making me, they would only say that they were trying to get the best possible outcome and that the ball was in the prosecutor's court. They made it clear that they didn't want to risk alienating the prosecutors and there was nothing anyone could say to change their minds. My mom and I were highly frustrated and on opposite sides of this issue with my dad, who said we had to respect our lawyers' decision. For a while, this created a deep divide within our family.

Four-and-a-half months had now passed since my trip to Washington without hearing anything from the prosecutors. Emotionally, my parents and I were at the end of our rope. My anxiety level was off the charts and I was incapable of talking about anything else and paralyzed with fear. Finally, my attorneys became sufficiently uncomfortable with this delay and initiated a call to the prosecutors. Ken reached one of them, who said that the FBI psychologist's conclusions were the following: he agreed with all our experts' findings; he didn't believe I posed a threat to children; and he had no objection to my being given diversion.

In spite of the FBI psychologist agreeing with our experts, the prosecutors would still not change their position. My lawyers were very upset and asked if they could read the report that the FBI psychologist had written, but were told the prosecutors had never even requested one. That was confusing. Why would the prosecutors send me to this expert but not want a written report from him? The FBI psychologist had clearly told my dad and me that he would write a report if asked to do so.

After waiting so long and getting such bad news, my parents and I were crushed. My mom and dad both broke down and cried. None of it made any sense. I had done exactly what the prosecutors had asked me to do, and now they were ignoring their own expert's conclusions.

Feeling very frustrated, my lawyers requested a meeting with the US Attorney who supervised the lawyers who were prosecuting me. This meeting took place on May 7, 2012, and was attended by my lawyers, the US Attorney, the criminal chief of the division, one of the FBI agents who had raided my apartment, and the two prosecutors who had been working on my case. After the meeting, my lawyers called to report the outcome. They said the US Attorney had agreed to read my file and review the proposed plea offer to determine whether that offer should stand or diversion should be given. My lawyers saw this as a good sign and felt that there was now some hope for diversion.

Four hours later, Ken received a surprising call from the prosecutors saying that the US Attorney had requested that I have yet another evaluation from a forensic psychologist who regularly testified in high-profile criminal cases for the prosecutor's office. This sudden request troubled my lawyers for a couple of reasons. First, the prosecutors had previously assured my lawyers that if I was examined by the FBI neuropsychologist in Washington DC they would not need anything further to come to their decision. Second, because this forensic psychologist had no background in Asperger's/autism, they were very concerned he would not understand the nuances of this case.

My lawyers vigorously expressed their concerns to the prosecutors, but to no avail. Either I went through another grueling examination with someone who lacked expertise in Asperger's/autism, or I would be indicted, which would put me on the trial docket.

My mother termed this agonizing decision a "Sophie's Choice," because both options were equally terrible. My trip to Washington was still a recent trauma and the thought of going through another long and intensely probing interrogation filled me with dread. Again, I sought advice from those I trusted. Although everyone understood my tremendous reluctance, they felt it was my only hope for diversion. Katie was the one exception and tried to discourage me from doing it. Being an expert in autism herself, she was very worried about a psychologist examining me who didn't have any background in the subject. She also worried that if this interview didn't go well, it could bring prison back on the table. She said that she didn't want me playing Russian roulette with my life. She and I were on the same wavelength, as prison was also my greatest fear. Against my better judgment, I decided to do the interview. I just hoped it would be scheduled quickly and I could get it over with soon. No such luck.

For the next five months I waited to hear from the prosecutors regarding the scheduling of an appointment with the forensic psychologist. This delay was utterly maddening as, again, there seemed to be no discernable reason for it. If the prosecutors wanted this examination, why hadn't they contacted this guy already? I felt as if I were going insane. My lawyers then decided to contact the doctor directly, but he said he couldn't schedule an appointment with me until the prosecutors had hired him. Finally, the prosecutors sent an email stating that this forensic psychologist would see me in three weeks. All the previous reports were sent to him, but, of course, there was no written report from the FBI neuropsychologist that could be included.

My appointment was on a dreary Michigan, autumn day. Once again, I felt as if this was the most important meeting of my life and that the rest of my days on earth could hinge on the success or failure of this interview. That was a lot of pressure to feel, especially for the second time in one year.

As my dad and I walked into his office, the forensic psychologist made it clear he had no interest in talking with my father. This was unlike the interview with the FBI neuropsychologist, where my dad was invited in for a brief period to talk about his experiences of parenting a special needs child.

This examiner showed no emotion whatsoever and had an intimidating presence. He began the interview in the same way the FBI neuropsychologist had, by telling me he had been retained by the prosecutors and anything I said could be used against me. He also told me he could be called upon to testify against me in court. Was I willing to accept this and proceed? What choice did I have?

He grilled me like a seasoned detective trying to piece together the reasons why I had committed this offense. One thing that disturbed me was that none of his questions had anything to do with autism or Asperger's. Unlike the FBI neuropsychologist who was very cognizant of my disability and wanted me to describe how it impacted my daily life, this doctor showed no such interest. Whatever questions he asked, I answered them honestly. Many of his questions involved my most intimate thoughts and were humiliating for me to answer, but I knew I had to be completely honest with him.

The interview lasted six hours. After that, he administered the MMPI, the same test I had taken with Dr Maltz. Again, the test showed I did not have psychopathic tendencies but it did show elevations for both depression and anxiety that apparently had increased since the last time I had taken the test. That came as no surprise. The events of the last year had taken a tremendous toll on me.

A month after the evaluation, the forensic psychologist sent his written report to the prosecutors and to my attorneys. His report stated that I had been honest with him and he did not consider me to be a threat to children. He agreed with all of the other experts that there was a correlation between my lack of social and sexual development and viewing child pornography. He also didn't think I should be prosecuted for a crime that would place me on the sex offender registry.

Ken was happy with his report but his enthusiasm was short lived. A few weeks later, the US Attorney and staff of prosecutors held a meeting to decide my case, once and for all. My lawyers were not permitted to attend. In the end, the US Attorney decided to give me the same plea deal they had offered a year-and-a-half earlier: no prison, but a felony conviction and registration as a sex offender.

I felt very sad and defeated. The prosecution had irrevocably closed the door on diversion and there was nothing left to do. I either had to take the plea or go to trial. Going to trial was not an option for me. I was emotionally drained from the past two-and-a-half years and knew that I could not handle any further involvement with the criminal justice system. I was formally indicted.

Six weeks later, in front of the presiding federal judge, I entered a guilty plea for one count possession of child pornography. It was another humiliating experience that I wouldn't wish on anyone, although the judge handled it as gracefully and sensitively as possible. My sentencing date was scheduled for three months later, so I had another agonizing waiting period ahead of me.

The day of my sentencing finally arrived. Even though I was hopeful that the plea agreement would go through, I was still worried that the judge technically had the authority to set aside the plea and send me to prison. Fifteen minutes before the hearing began, Dr Green unexpectedly showed up to support me. I was so glad to see my therapist and he gave me a much-needed hug. The only people in the courtroom were my parents, Ken, Dr Green, the prosecutor, and me. I found it interesting that throughout the entire time we were there, the prosecutor avoided making eye contact with my parents or me.

The proceedings were to begin at 2:30 p.m., but the judge was delayed for half an hour. It was eerily quiet in the courtroom as we all sat waiting for the judge to take the bench. My parents and I seemed to be lost in our own thoughts. Two-and-a-half years of uncertainty, delays, and unimaginable fear had led up to this moment in time. As the bailiff's voice boomed out, "The United States of America v. Nicolas Dubin," the judge entered the courtroom. Everyone rose. My face was beet red and I was sweating profusely. I stood at the podium directly in front of the judge.

After some preliminary remarks, the judge asked me if I had anything to say to the court. I said I was very sorry for the actions that had led me to come before this court and I felt great shame for the pain I had caused my family. I assured the judge that I had been seeing a therapist twice a week since my arrest and that I took my treatment very seriously. I ended by saying that I felt great remorse and hoped to help the Asperger's autism community learn from my mistakes in whatever way I could and that I would never commit this offense again. The judge looked me in the eye and said he believed me. He said that although I was originally charged with distribution, it was clear I never distributed this material and if he thought I had, he would have sentenced me to a long term in prison. He also acknowledged the degree of punishment I had already endured from this story being in the media as well as being on a tether for two-and-a-half years.

The judge then accepted the plea agreement and put me on supervised release for five years, which was by law the minimum he could have given me. He said that in reading all the reports that had been submitted to him, he had learned something new: that Asperger's syndrome was a neurological condition, not a mental illness. I was surprised to hear him say this. I would have expected someone as educated and seasoned as a federal judge to know this basic fact. It confirmed to me that the legal system has a lot of catching up to do when it comes to learning about autism spectrum disorders.

Then, he wished me good luck and I breathed a sigh of relief. My family's long and tortuous battle with the federal government had suddenly come to an end. My parents and I were physically and emotionally drained, but we were glad this part of the journey was finally over. After two-and-a-half years of intense and unrelenting struggle, I would now be faced with the daunting task of trying to rebuild my life.

Afterword

With few exceptions, people on the autism spectrum do not belong in the criminal justice system. They are highly moral and extremely law-abiding individuals. That is how I would describe myself now and how I would have described myself at the time of my arrest. Yet I unwittingly committed a very serious crime. How did this happen and how has it happened to others on the autism spectrum? In order to answer these questions, light needs to be shed on a subject that has not been given sufficient attention: autism and sexuality. My hope in writing this portion of the book has been to create awareness and a jumping-off place for a discussion to begin on a long-neglected subject.

It must first be acknowledged that most people on the autism spectrum are sexual beings who don't have the same sexual outlets throughout their development as their neurotypical counterparts. At some point, this lack of sexual knowledge and experience can create a variety of problems. This developmental difference is the "elephant in the room" that no one wants to talk about.

At the time of my arrest, I considered myself somewhat of an expert in Asperger's syndrome. I had earned a doctoral degree in psychology and all of my research, writings, and internships were in that area of study. I had also authored several books, produced three DVDs, and given numerous speeches, all involving different aspects of having Asperger's syndrome. In spite of my total immersion in the subject, I still had no awareness of the potential problems that some people with Asperger's, including myself, can have as a result of their sexual development.

Since my diagnosis, I have read every book I could get my hands on regarding autism and Asperger's syndrome. With the exception of Dr Isabelle Hénault's *Asperger's and Sexuality*, I found almost nothing on the subject, other than "how-to-date" books. Over the past two years, I have often wondered if I had read a book like the one I am now writing, whether I could have avoided this disastrous predicament.

Based on my personal experience, I would like to offer some thoughts and suggestions to different groups of people, including parents of those on the autism spectrum, mental health professionals, and those involved in the criminal justice system. In order to prevent situations like the one I experienced from ever happening again, these groups need to have certain vital information. I hope my story will serve as a cautionary tale. I don't want anyone on the spectrum or his/her family to endure the degree of suffering my parents and I have over the past two-and-a-half years or bear the stigma of the sex offender registry and the social and employment restrictions I will face for the rest of my life.

Parents of children (whatever their age) on the spectrum

My parents tried their best to get me to talk about dating and sex, but I was a very fierce opponent. Whenever they dared to bring up anything regarding my social life or sexuality, it was like touching a hot stove. I would become defensive and shut them down immediately. I refused to talk about those areas of my life with them or anyone else, which ultimately did not serve me well. In fact, it contributed to my demise. Because I would not address it, my sexuality became frozen in time for many years. I was too afraid to deal with it and was able to keep my parents from helping me to deal with it. I understand that it is uncomfortable to force a child to talk about something so personal, especially when there is resistance. Attempting to talk to any child about his or her sexuality can be awkward, but for someone on the spectrum, it may be exponentially more difficult. But if parents put their heads in the sand for too long, the consequences can be devastating, not only for their child, but also for the entire family.

I know that it is painful to realize and to accept that your child is socially and sexually progressing differently from other children. It can be frustrating when a teenager is not interested in dating or going to parties, but it is important not to force the issue, like my mother tried to do before my diagnosis. Parents seem to fall into two camps when it comes to their concern for their child's social/sexual development: those who try to pressure their children into having more of a social life and those who ignore the subject altogether. The latter is usually the path of least resistance. Parents often think, "Why look for trouble? My child has enough problems to deal with so why add another thing to the list?"

As I have come to learn, the internet can be a wonderful educational tool and it can also ruin your life. If a child is spending too much time on the computer, a parent should try to make sure nothing inappropriate is taking place. These days, especially for those on the spectrum who often spend an inordinate amount of time on their computers, it has become far too easy to explore one's sexuality in total isolation using the internet. When someone has little to no social or sexual experience, visiting certain websites can become a poor substitute. If parents suspect their child is using the internet inappropriately, they can install filtering software on their child's computer regarding sexual material. They should also seek professional help immediately, but often the question is—from whom?

I live in a large metropolitan area, and yet my parents could not find a therapist with expertise in both Asperger's *and* sexuality. Ultimately, they had to choose someone with a specialty in one of these areas (sexuality) and hope that he would educate himself in Asperger's. Having knowledge in both areas is essential to helping an autistic client deal with his/her sexual issues but, unfortunately, few such people exist. Therefore, it is critical for a therapist working with autistic clients to become knowledgeable about how their sexual development may be different from the neurotypicals they normally treat.

Psychologists, social workers, and other mental health professionals

Most therapists who treat autistic clients are overwhelmed by the sheer number of psychological, emotional, and daily living problems their clients face. It is very easy to put sexuality on the backburner when a client doesn't bring the issue up and is also experiencing profound depression, anxiety, social alienation, unemployment, strained family relationships, and other mental health issues. In the past two years, I have spoken with several psychologists who work with Asperger's adults and they report that their clients are reluctant to talk about their sexuality, which makes it difficult for them, as therapists, to broach the subject.

Some autistic clients will talk endlessly about wanting a girlfriend, but that kind of discussion usually stays on a superficial level. Clients with Asperger's will often try to keep the conversation general and avoid the sexual turmoil that may be going on beneath the surface. Embarrassment or a simple lack of understanding of the inappropriateness of a behavior may prevent them from disclosing any of the inappropriate sexual behaviors in which they might be engaging. Therapists may have to gently scratch the surface before they can dig deeper and get to the heart of the matter. This process may take months and requires patience and persistence. There is always the danger that a client may quit therapy if the therapist is perceived as being too intrusive, so the therapist must walk a fine line.

If a client admits to some inappropriate sexual behavior, like I did, it is crucial for the therapist to regularly follow up on it. The implications and possible consequences of the behavior must be clearly and repeatedly spelled out. Autistic clients also need to understand how their inappropriate sexual behavior affects others. This type of explanation may be unnecessary with neurotypicals, but must be hammered away at with someone on the spectrum. Besides explaining the negative effects to the client, the therapist can also try to stop the inappropriate and possibly illegal sexual behavior. If the issue is viewing child pornography, a therapist can make a contract with the client to ensure he will cease the behavior, and then regularly follow up to make sure the contract is being honored. Similar contracts can be made with clients regarding stalking, inappropriate sexual touching, or exposing oneself.

A therapist should understand that, for an autistic person, inappropriate sexual touching is often caused by hyposensitivity, a need for stimulation as a result of being under stimulated. In an earlier chapter, I mentioned that throughout my childhood, I would touch people's heads. This behavior was certainly strange, but not harmful or sexually offensive and I was only a child. However, when an autistic child grows up and becomes an adult, this need for stimulation combined with the lack of a sexual outlet, can create the perfect storm for inappropriate sexual touching and can lead to unwanted and serious consequences.

People on the spectrum are rarely sexual predators or pedophiles. In fact, they tend to be the victims of crimes rather than the perpetrators.

They simply have a different psychosexual development from their neurotypical counterparts and this difference can sometimes affect interpersonal relationships and encounters with strangers, as well as sexual exploration that can take place on the computer.

To this day, I am still in therapy with Dr Green. He is an excellent psychologist and we have a solid rapport. He has been a huge source of support in helping me cope with numerous post-arrest challenges. He says that working with me has been like a graduate course in Asperger's. We have both learned a lot from each other since my arrest. I have made a lot of progress in my therapy during this time and he has learned a great deal about working with people on the autism spectrum.

Professionals in the criminal justice system

Other than getting a traffic ticket, I never had any contact with the police before my arrest. I believe it is important for law enforcement to have some basic training focusing on how to confront or arrest someone on the spectrum. Most people on the spectrum are not dangerous as long as they know they will not be physically threatened or harmed.

People with Asperger's can sometimes look suspicious to the police as a result of behaviors that fall outside conventional norms. For example, an officer might interpret lack of eye contact as a sign of deception or a meltdown as a physical threat. These behaviors need to be taken into account so that a situation doesn't escalate and have an unfortunate outcome. A judge could also misinterpret certain behaviors, such as smirking, nervous laughter, and lack of eye contact, as a defendant not taking the proceedings seriously or showing a lack of respect for the court, when such behavior actually stems from the person's nervous system being taxed beyond its endurance by high levels of anxiety and fear.

When speaking to an autistic person, police officers should give very clear, direct instructions in a calm and modulated voice while still ensuring their own safety. They should also be aware that it is not uncommon for those on the spectrum to be arrested for something they didn't know was illegal, so the arrest may come as a shock, as it did for me. Although the FBI would have known I had Asperger's, they entered my apartment with the same degree of force necessary to apprehend Al Capone. The impact of twelve agents bursting into my apartment was very psychologically damaging to me beyond what words can articulate. I believe the sazme goal could have been achieved in a more peaceful and humane way.

Those in the criminal justice system who are involved in sentencing must understand that people with Asperger's/autism have certain deficits that make prison life even more intolerable than it is for neurotypicals. For example: they would have great difficulty understanding the social cues and the politics of what is needed to get along with others; they couldn't possibly join a gang in order to get protection; they might unwittingly say the wrong thing to someone in authority and get in serious trouble; and the sensory issues, including the constant noises of inmates yelling, cell doors shutting, and bright lights, would be completely overwhelming. If an autistic person absolutely needs to be detained, house arrest is a far better alternative.

The best advice I could give defense lawyers with an autistic client is to do research and learn how this disorder may have contributed to the crime in question. It is safe to assume that prosecutors will have little if any understanding of autism and it is the defense lawyer's job to educate not only him/herself, but also the prosecutor. As primers, I would suggest Dr Tony Attwood's two informative and comprehensive books on Asperger's syndrome (Attwood 1997, 2008).

Asperger's/autism by itself, and excluding any existing co-morbidities, is not a mental illness. It is a neurological disorder that impacts behavior from birth and makes it difficult for a person to read social cues. People with Asperger's process information differently. Any crime that involves a social or cognitive misunderstanding, including stalking, harassment, disturbing the peace (because of a meltdown), possessing child pornography, inappropriate sexual touching, hacking into well-secured government or corporate databases for the curiosity of it, or stealing merchandise related to one's special interest may be related in part to being autistic. If an attorney suspects that Asperger's or autism relates to the offense in question, it is important for that attorney to get medical, psychological, and educational reports that corroborate the client's symptoms as far back as possible, even if no current diagnosis exists.

Defense lawyers tend to focus solely on the crime a client is charged with and often fail to take into account how autism might play a role in the client's culpability. Lawyers need to take the time to understand how a neurological deficit may be related to the crime with which the client is charged. In the absence of taking this time, the outcome of the case may seem reasonable to the defense attorney but, in fact, could be unfair to the autistic client.

Lawyers also need to know that clients on the spectrum may require more communication than most clients. I suggest lawyers be as clear and direct as possible and make sure their client understands exactly what has been said. Also, it is helpful to understand how autistic people tend to process information. For example, if a lawyer says that a particular thing is going to happen, that will create a definite expectation, so if there is any change in plan, the client may become upset or frustrated. If that situation occurs, the lawyer should understand the client's difficulty in adapting to change, try to show him/her some empathy, and explain the reason(s) why the change was necessary. This kind of communication takes a little extra time that busy lawyers don't always have but that autistic clients really need.

My lawyers spent a great deal of time establishing good relationships with all the members of my family, which I think is very important to do. If attorneys establish good communication with the client's parents, spouse, or siblings, they will get a lot more information than the client alone may be able to provide.

And finally, here are my thoughts to prosecutors. I am grateful that the prosecutors in my case decided to take prison off the table because they clearly saw that I was not a predator. If they had any doubt, I would be in prison right now. While I appreciate their decision, I also wish that they had followed the opinions of the experts, including their own, who believed I should not have been criminally prosecuted and forced to register as a sex offender. I realize that it takes courage for a prosecutor, whose primary job is to seek convictions, not to prosecute but instead to exercise prosecutorial discretion when the circumstances are justified, as a means to achieve justice.

Final thoughts

For the rest of my life, I will continue to be sorry to three groups of people: the children whose pictures I viewed without realizing the harm I was causing them; my family, for subjecting them to the worst experience a child can put their parents through; and the Asperger's community, who I always hoped to represent in a positive way.

I have learned a lot about myself during what has been the most painful experience of my life. As a result of extensive therapy, I am trying to come to terms with the guilt and shame I have carried with me since middle school. I have also learned to be honest with myself. I should have dealt with my sexuality a long time ago, but it was too scary for me and I buried it. Others on the spectrum may fall victim to this kind of denial, and I pray that this book helps in some way to prevent that.

I am an extremely private person who would never have thought that I would some day be sharing information about my sexual development with the general public. During the writing of this book, I have been continually asking myself why I am doing this and here is what the tipping point was for me. My father received a call from a parent of a young man with autism who is serving time in federal prison for possession of child pornography. He has been constantly bullied, physically assaulted by other inmates, and placed in solitary confinement by guards who misinterpret his behavior. Sadly, there is nothing his family can do about it. I am writing this book in the hope that others on the autism spectrum will not have to be subjected to such horrific treatment in the future.

Emily Dickinson wrote a poem entitled, "I Shall Not Live In Vain." Perhaps this poem sums up what I have attempted to do in writing this book.

If I can stop one heart from breaking,
I shall not live in vain;
If I can ease one life the aching,
Or cool one pain,
Or help one fainting robin
Unto his nest again,
I shall not live in vain.

References

Attwood, T. (2008) *The Complete Guide to Asperger's Syndrome.* London: Jessica Kingsley Publishers.

Attwood, T. (1997) *Asperger's Syndrome: A Guide for Parents and Professionals.* London: Jessica Kingsley Publishers.

AN EXPERT'S VIEW

Tony Attwood

The Pathway to Accessing Child Pornography

I have met Nick at his home in the United States and concur that he has the classic characteristics and developmental history of an adult who has Asperger's syndrome. Unfortunately, he was a child in an age when clinicians were unaware of the distinct pattern of abilities we now recognize as part of the autism spectrum. His diagnosis was delayed until he was twenty-seven, thus he missed out on the opportunity for understanding, guidance and support from specialists in Asperger's syndrome during his adolescence, particularly in the important area of social and sexual development. This has been a major factor in his pathway to an interest in pornography and, eventually, child pornography.

It is important that parents and clinicians and those who have Asperger's syndrome learn from Nick's experiences. This will not only act as a deterrent to following the same path, but also an encouragement to achieve greater and more successful social inclusion with peers, provide effective sexuality education and increase self-acceptance, which will be of great benefit to all those who have Asperger's syndrome.

Nick is an honest and brave young man and his decision to explain his experiences, emotions and thoughts so that others may avoid the same pathway is to be applauded. From my clinical experience, Nick's case of someone with Asperger's syndrome accessing child pornography is not unique. This chapter will explore, from a clinician's perspective, the complex background factors related to Asperger's syndrome that led to his arrest. However, it is important to state that an interest in illegal pornography is not an anticipated characteristic of adolescents and adults who have Asperger's syndrome. So why did Nick develop this interest that culminated in his arrest for committing a serious criminal offence?

There are many factors that explain his behaviour, in particular: his social isolation; social and sexual immaturity; lack of accurate information on sexuality; and low self-esteem, and vulnerability to anxiety and depression.

Social isolation

Children who have Asperger's syndrome have considerable difficulty understanding social conventions and making friends, which makes them conspicuously different to their peers. Some typical children can be remarkably kind and tolerant of someone who is different, but in every class and playground there will be children who enjoy tormenting, teasing, rejecting and humiliating the child with Asperger's syndrome. Children who have Asperger's syndrome often desperately seek inclusion, acceptance and respect from their peers, but usually experience alienation and ridicule. For example, Nick refers to his not making a single friend in all three years of middle school. Temporary isolation is very difficult for any child to cope with, but the extreme social isolation he experienced throughout his childhood had a devastating effect on Nick's self-esteem.

A child who is socially isolated can provide some self-comfort by escaping into imagination, an alternative world of social success. The imaginary scenes become vivid and entrancing and are an effective retreat from a painful reality. In the adult years, solitary imaginative activities can become a way of achieving almost another persona that does not have the characteristics and vulnerabilities of Asperger's syndrome. Imagination can also be used to explore and repair events and experiences from childhood, such as being bullied and rejected. This became a factor in Nick's pathway to accessing child pornography.

Bullying and teasing

It was not simply that Nick could not find the elusive, genuine friendship he sought, or that he felt lonely; it was that he also experienced almost daily bullying, teasing, humiliation and rejection. This had a devastating effect on his self-esteem and the development of his social and, eventually, sexual maturity. The bullying was not restricted to his classroom and playground experiences, but wherever he met his peers and older and younger children. He felt increasingly that he was different and defective and this intense feeling of shame became a contributory factor to the development of a clinical depression. He became self-critical, internalizing his despair. His peers were quite simply toxic to his mental health, such that he experienced high levels of anxiety whenever he was expected to interact with them. However, he could retreat to his home, which became a safe "castle" away from the "war zone," but peer-imposed and self-imposed isolation for survival had a significant inhibitory effect on his social maturity. He became a hermit.

It is also apparent in Nick's childhood that he tended to suffer in silence. He was an easy target, unlikely to retaliate and he was remarkably well behaved at school, considering his inner turmoil. His teachers may not have been aware of the psychological effect of bullying on Nick; nevertheless, his parents would have seen the effect, ranging from depression to anger, at home. It would be heartbreaking to see such suffering, yet be unable to protect your child when he is with his peers. Nick was very courageous in going to school each day, knowing he was going to be "ambushed" by the predators. Many children with Asperger's syndrome who experience such bullying are suspended from school for retaliating or develop school refusal.

Often, typical girls have compassion for the lonely and vulnerable boy with Asperger's syndrome, and may offer inclusion in their activities and conversation. They may help by being able to contradict the torments and repair the low self-esteem resulting from derogatory comments of the predatory peers. Nick was unusual for a boy with Asperger's syndrome in that, throughout his childhood and adolescence, he was not "adopted" by girls. This both compounded his loneliness and meant that he did not have the counterbalance that friendship with the opposite gender can provide to being bullied and teased. However, Nick did have his pets as friends. Animals are loyal, safe, trustworthy and pleased to see and play with their owner, but they cannot compensate fully for being rejected, bullied and teased by peers.

Talking about feelings

One of the characteristics of Asperger's syndrome is a difficulty with self-reflection, that is, conceptualizing and disclosing inner thoughts and feelings. As a clinician, I often have to help children or adolescents develop a "vocabulary" of words that accurately describe their inner feelings. Even if Nick had a close friend, he would still have had difficulty translating his complex inner world into conversational speech. This would have further compounded his loneliness and significantly inhibited his ability to seek guidance and understanding. As with many children and adolescents with Asperger's syndrome, he would have had great difficulty opening his heart to friends and family.

Puberty and sexuality

Nick's reclusive life provided a safe sanctuary within his home and within his private inner world, but his isolation was clearly delaying his social development. It would not, however, delay the onset of puberty. Nick would have the typical sexual responses of a teenager but no opportunity to discuss his thoughts and experiences with supportive peers. Typical adolescents are able to share with each other their thoughts, feelings and experiences, and offer each other reassurance that most of these new sensations, thoughts and bodily changes are a normal, natural part of puberty and growing up.

Some of the new thoughts would concern the development of a romantic interest in someone, and herald the start of the adolescent's progression along the continuum of intimacy. When I talk to young adults who have Asperger's syndrome, they often describe having the sensory response but not the same relationship experiences as their peers. They tend to experience a significant delay in the development of romantic relationships, which can be by circumstances or choice.

Often, the person with Asperger's syndrome is not "cool" or attractive to peers in early adolescence. Indeed, many adolescents with Asperger's syndrome actually and accurately feel too young for a romantic relationship, are unsure and immature regarding dating, and appear to peers as overly prudish. There may actually be a preference for being asexual, that is, not interested in an intimate relationship with anyone, male or female. This can be due to their feeling vulnerable to teasing about romantic attachments, not being able to identify dishonourable intentions, being unsure of the codes of romantic conduct and preferring autonomy. It may feel safer to be celibate. It is interesting that a greater than expected proportion of adults with Asperger's syndrome consciously choose to be celibate throughout their lives for any or all of these reasons.

Sometimes the delay in an apparent interest in sexuality, especially among adolescent boys who regularly talk about girls and their attributes, can lead to accusations of, "If you are not interested, you must be gay," irrespective of whether the person has developed a gender preference in relationships. This can be very confusing for an adolescent who has Asperger's syndrome who is in the process of discovering his or her own sexuality. Unfortunately, the clear message is that being gay is unacceptable within that group of peers.

In many cultures, these are certain aspects of sexuality that are perceived primarily in terms of preserving innocence, and consequently it becomes a topic that is too confronting or uncomfortable for a parent or teacher to discuss. If the adolescent with Asperger's syndrome is not gaining positive and accurate information on sexuality from parents, teachers, close friends or early romantic experiences, where do they go for the information?

For most adolescents with Asperger's syndrome, the computer has provided, since early childhood, valuable information, recreation and enjoyment. The internet is a link to the outside world from the safety of home and becomes almost a substitute "friend." Where there is curiosity regarding sexual experiences, the internet will be the adolescent's guide, and pornography becomes the tutor. Adolescents and young adults who have Asperger's syndrome have few interpersonal pleasures in their lives, and private sexual fantasies explored on the internet would provide information and enjoyment.

One of the characteristics of Asperger's syndrome is the development of a special interest. Each interest has a "use by date," from hours to decades, and often involves collecting and cataloguing information. From my clinical experience, many adolescent males with Asperger's syndrome develop an interest in pornography. While this is a characteristic of many typical adolescent and adult males, the interest for those with Asperger's syndrome can be at a much greater depth, in terms of time spent looking at pornography and the type of pornography. For the person with Asperger's syndrome, the enjoyment occurs in a situation where there is no risk of rejection, as can occur in real life, and there is a sense of being in control and safe from humiliation. There can then be a determination to eventually explore all aspects of pornography, to "complete the collection." This can lead to an intellectual curiosity regarding aspects of pornography that are illegal. For many of the adolescents and adults I have known charged with the same offence as Nick, there is the erroneous belief that access to such internet sites is undetectable and not illegal, the activity occurring in the privacy of one's own home without harm to anyone. However, the police can detect access, especially to child pornography sites. Accessing child pornography is a crime, since there is, in fact, a clear victim, that is, the child in the photograph or video.

Homosexuality

Those with Asperger's syndrome tend to be late developers, not only in terms of social and emotional maturity but also in terms of sexuality. They need time to sort out issues such as self-identity, and the opportunity to have positive and supportive experiences in friendships with both genders. Although Nick tried to "flip the heterosexual switch" he was not successful, so his sexuality went underground, eventually emerging as having homosexual thoughts.

Child pornography

Asperger's syndrome is a condition of contradictions in abilities, often referred to as asynchronous development. This uneven profile of development creates considerable confusion for others who have difficulty understanding how someone with Asperger's syndrome can be highly intelligent yet display significant developmental delay in other areas. This was certainly the case with Nick. Despite his intellectual ability, Nick was significantly delayed in his social, sexual and emotional abilities. This was in part due to his social isolation inhibiting maturity, but clinicians recognize that developmental delay in these areas does seem to be a constitutional component of Asperger's syndrome. Formal testing of his adaptive functioning, that is, daily living skills, estimated his developmental level was at a level of a pre-adolescent.

Nick's pre-adolescent sexuality was frozen in time. However, there was another dimension. He wanted to return to the simpler life of childhood, to gain the acceptance and friendships he had never had with his peers as a child. He sought to repair the traumas of rejection and bullying. Once again, he escaped into an imaginary world, but this was the world of child pornography, access to which is illegal. One of the characteristics of Asperger's syndrome is confusion regarding social and sexuality boundaries, and Nick did not recognize the clear moral and legal boundaries.

Additional factors

Two further significant characteristics of Asperger's syndrome would have had a direct impact on Nick's viewing of child pornography. Psychologists use the term "impaired Theory of Mind" to describe a difficulty in understanding and appreciating the perspective, thoughts and experiences of another person. Nick would have had greater difficulty than a typical adult appreciating the perspective and experiences of the child in the photograph or movie. There would have been a sense of emotional detachment while he was viewing these images on his computer. The other characteristic "is impaired executive functioning," a term used by psychologists to describe difficulties with planning and organization, understanding a wider perspective and flexibility in problem solving, along with a single-minded determination to acquire information. Nick would have had difficulty appreciating the broader perspective of his actions and consequences to himself, tending to "live in the now" rather than, "What would happen if…?" He failed to see the broader picture.

Another factor is that, while he felt he was a child in an adult's body, he also had no idea how to be physically intimate with someone of his own chronological age. He lacked knowledge and experience regarding age-appropriate relationships, such that he could not progress along the continuum of intimacy in reality.

Nick also had periodic depression, and this would have deprived him of the energy and confidence to be more constructive regarding aspects of his sexuality and sexual interests. Thus, he was trapped and isolated in so many ways.

Strategies and Resources

We can gather so much valuable information from Nick's journey along the pathway to accessing child pornography in order to prevent other adults with Asperger's syndrome following the same path. These are some key preventative strategies.

Guidance and support in friendship abilities

Nick felt alienated from his peers and unable to make friends. This inhibited his social, and subsequently his sexual, development. Children and adolescents with Asperger's syndrome cannot be expected simply to watch other children and just try harder to be accepted and make friends. They need guidance and support in reading social situations and understanding the anticipated codes of social conduct of children their age, and tuition in the skills needed to develop and maintain friendships. This is not an easy task, but it is an essential one when a child has a diagnosis of Asperger's syndrome. It is important that other children are given guidance in how to constructively and positively include a child with Asperger's syndrome in their activities in the playground and the classroom. It is also important to build confidence by commending the child with Asperger's syndrome when he or she demonstrates particular friendship skills and to commend the other children for successful inclusion.

Guidance in social conventions can be achieved by the use of Social Stories™ and Comic Strip Conversations developed by Carol Gray, and adolescents can use role play and drama activities to rehearse what to do in specific situations, from conversation skills to the dating game.

There will also need to be guidance in reading body language and in the expected codes of social conduct. It can be valuable to engage the help of several children who act as mentors and guardians to provide support and protection when the teacher is busy.

Fortunately, we now have programs that can be used by teachers, clinicians and parents to improve friendship abilities throughout childhood and adolescence. Nick did not have access to resources and expertise on friendship during his childhood, and thus he suffered isolation and loneliness, which inhibited and disrupted his social and sexual development.

The prevention of bullying

A 2012 survey of eight thousand people with autism, conducted by the National Autistic Society in the United Kingdom, found that 82 per cent of young people with high-functioning autism or Asperger's syndrome had been bullied. Thus, bullying is an anticipated experience for the vast majority of children and adolescents with Asperger's syndrome. Being bullied, rejected, teased and humiliated had a devastating effect on Nick's self-esteem, making social interactions with his peers fraught with anxiety, and contributing to his clinical depression and subsequent escape into imagination and solitary pursuits.

The taunts included accusations of being gay, a currently popular derogatory term for someone who is different and perceived as weird. The predators probably sensed this was a sensitive topic for Nick, and thus had more enjoyment from his confusion and distress. This also affected his emerging sexuality and compounded his inability to confide in a friend for support.

Schools are becoming more aware of the consequences of bullying on both typical children and adolescents, and on those with Asperger's syndrome. From my clinical experience, the consequence of bullying can be lethal and has been a major contributory factor for attempted suicide in adolescents with Asperger's syndrome. While home is a safe "castle" with protection from the predators, it can become a prison, where escape is through the internet.

There are many programs to prevent bullying, but they need to be adapted for the thinking and life experiences of those with

Asperger's syndrome. As most acts of bullying are not witnessed by a teacher, an essential component of an anti-bullying program is for the "silent majority," who are not victims or predators, to step in and stop them, clearly stating that such behaviour will not be tolerated and *will* be reported. Peers need to be empowered and encouraged to be part of the prevention program. It is also important to explain to the child, perhaps using a Social Story™, the psychology of predators, since he or she often cannot understand why a person would actually enjoy being cruel to someone who is inoffensive. It seems illogical. The program should also encourage the child or adolescent with Asperger's syndrome to be assertive, stay calm and not take the hurtful comments to heart. Teachers and parents will need to monitor the risk of particular children being bullied, as those with Asperger's syndrome can be reluctant to disclose what is happening. Teachers and parents will also need to provide an opportunity for the child or adolescent to "de-brief" after being bullied, to facilitate recovery and closure. Finally, it is interesting to note that Nick has written an excellent book on strategies and solutions to bullying, based on his own experiences.

Guidance on aspects of puberty and sexuality

Puberty is a time of change in the adolescent's body, thinking, abilities and emotional range and intensity. It is also a time of change in the nature of conversations and friendships, and may herald the emergence of romantic relationships. Generally, people who have Asperger's syndrome do not like change, and the consequences of puberty can be confusion, anxiety and low self-esteem. The antidote is accurate, age-appropriate information, and support and reassurance from parents and peers. This should commence early in the child's life and include clear and unambiguous education about private and public places, activities and body parts, and boundaries for behaviour of each stage of childhood and adolescence.

During the pre-puberty years, the child will need to be well informed of the body changes that are to be expected for both boys and girls and the importance of self-care in terms of personal hygiene, diet, exercise, recreation and sleep. The changes are then not a surprise and can be accepted and welcomed. As puberty progresses, it is essential to have regular open and honest discussions, with information on relationships and normal sexual feelings. This provides reassurance and increases confidence, and also helps the young person make wise choices in their sexual experiences and romantic relationships. Parents need to be honest and accurate in providing the information and always maintain the adolescent's confidentiality. They must be mindful that if they do not provide the information the adolescent seeks, he or she will get it instead from peers, who may take advantage of the adolescent's naivety and provide inappropriate or incorrect information, or from the internet, with the consequences experienced by Nick.

The guidance also needs to include discussion of sexual feelings towards opposite and same gender peers. Young adolescents going through the early stages of puberty may experiment with their same gender friends, viewing or touching each other's bodies, but this is a part of growing up and not necessarily an indication of being homosexual as an adult. Those who are genuinely homosexual are more likely to become sure of their gender preference for a partner in their late teens.

Recent research (soon to be published), conducted by Kat Stork-Brett in Australia, has examined sexuality and Asperger's syndrome in some detail, with a questionnaire completed by well over fifteen hundred respondents. Respondents' ages ranged from eighteen to eighty-two years and they were from all over the world. She found that people who have Asperger's syndrome are actually *less* likely than the typical population to be homosexual, although they do appear to identify significantly *more* as having an asexual orientation.

Adolescents with Asperger's syndrome also need guidance in the "dating game," for example: knowing when someone finds them attractive; what they can talk about with that person; where they can go on a first date; what would be appropriate in terms of touch; and understanding that there must be mutual agreement to progress along the continuum of intimacy. There also needs to be guidance on what experiences are legal at what age and how to avoid risky situations. If information is primarily from the internet, it is likely that the images will be from the extreme section of the intimacy continuum and will not provide information about what to do in the early stages of a relationship. Nick had little if any guidance from friends who were exploring the first stages of the intimacy continuum, thus once more he was isolated from his peers and their experiences, and anxious about his ability to have a relationship beyond that of platonic acquaintance.

As a parent, it is also common sense to have safeguards on all the computers in the house. It is important to remember that adolescents with Asperger's syndrome are often computer experts and will probably try to hide their tracks. Parents will need to check regularly which sites have been visited, and ensure their credit card details are not available to the adolescent. It is also important to clearly explain why the sites are prohibited and the potential consequences of accessing illegal sites. As Nick is an adult, it may have been assumed that he had the maturity to recognize the dangers in accessing illegal internet sites. However, it is important to consider the person's social and emotional maturity, rather than chronological age, and to explain why accessing child pornography is illegal, that there is a victim and what the legal and personal consequences would be for the person with Asperger's syndrome for accessing child pornography.

Self-acceptance

We are increasingly recognizing the lack of self-acceptance and low self-esteem of those with Asperger's syndrome as a contributory factor to further social isolation and depression. As a clinician, I am working with my colleagues at the Minds and Hearts clinic in Brisbane to develop and evaluate strategies for self-acceptance and adapt Cognitive Behaviour Therapy to treat depression in adolescents with Asperger's syndrome. If Nick had had greater self-confidence and energy, he may well have been able to avoid retreating into his world of imagination and the internet. It is important for clinicians treating someone with Asperger's syndrome for depression to also consider whether aspects of sexuality may be contributing to the depression. This was clearly the case for Nick, whose therapist overlooked how his troubled sexuality was fuelling his depression.

Acceptance by family members

Throughout all of Nick's trials and tribulations, including his arrest for accessing child pornography, his parents have maintained their love for and acceptance of their only child. I would like to commend his mother, and especially his father, for being so loyal, supportive and constructive. There were times when they were his only source of support. As they did not have a diagnosis until Nick was twenty-seven, they were also deprived of knowing where to go for professional guidance and support. Nick's parents have maintained their love for him and their faith in his abilities and personality. I share their faith in Nick, and I consider he is a hero for being so brave in revealing in this book his inner thoughts and experiences so that others do not follow the same path.

Training of psychologists and psychiatrists in sexuality and autism spectrum disorder

While there are psychologists and psychiatrists knowledgeable in autism spectrum disorders (ASDs), very few have expertise in sexuality and ASD. It is essential that clinicians consider and screen for aspects of sexuality when examining the origins of mood disorders, especially when treating adolescents. It is also important that forensic clinicians become knowledgeable in various aspects of ASD, not only in terms of screening clients for ASD, but also recognizing modifications to treatment programs, especially those for sex offenders, to incorporate issues associated with ASD such as difficulties with self-disclosure, alexithymia (marked dysfunction in emotional awareness, social attachment and interpersonal relating) and understanding the social codes in group therapy.

Recommended resources

Friendship abilities

Al-Ghani, K.I. (2011) *Learning About Friendship*. London: Jessica Kingsley Publishers.

Beaumont, R. (2010) *Secret Agent Society: Solving the Mystery of Social Encounters Program*. Milton, QLD: Social Skills Training Institute. More information at www.sst-institute.net.

Carter, M.A. and Santomauro, J. (2010) *Friendly Facts*. Shawnee Mission, KS: Autism Asperger Publishing Company.

Chasen, L.R. (2011) *Social Skills, Emotional Growth and Drama Therapy*. London: Jessica Kingsley Publishers.

Cook O'Toole, J. (2013) *The Asperkid's Secret Book of Social Rules*. London: Jessica Kingsley Publishers.

Cotugno, A.J. (2011) *Making Sense of Social Situations*. London: Jessica Kingsley Publishers.

Day, P. (2009) *What is friendship?* London: Jessica Kingsley Publishers.

Diamond, S. (2011) *Social Rules for Kids*. Shawnee Mission, KS: Autism Asperger Publishing Company.

Garcia Winner, M. (2000) *Inside Out: What Makes A Person With Social Cognitive Deficits Tick?* San Jose, CA: Think Social Publishing. More information at www.socialthinking.com.

Garcia Winner, M. and Crooke, P. (2011) *Socially Curious and Curiously Social*. San Jose, CA: Think Social Publishing; Great Barrington, MA: The North River Press Publishing Corporation.

Gray, C. (2010) *The New Social Story™ Book*. Arlington, TX: Future Horizons.

Lawson, W. (2006) *Friendships: The Aspie Way*. London: Jessica Kingsley Publishers.

McAfee, J. (2002) *Navigating the Social World*. Arlington, TX: Future Horizons.

Moyes, R. (2011) *Visual Techniques for Developing Social Skills*. Arlington, TX: Future Horizons.

Ordetx, K. (2012) *Teaching Theory of Mind*. London: Jessica Kingsley Publishers.

Painter, K.K. (2006) *Social Skills Groups for Children and Adolescents with Asperger's Syndrome*. London: Jessica Kingsley Publishers.

Plummer, D. (2005) *Helping Adolescents and Adults to Build Self-Esteem*. London: Jessica Kingsley Publishers.

Schneider, C.B. (2007) *Acting Antics*. London: Jessica Kingsley Publishers.

Schroeder, A. (2010) *The Friendship Formula*. Cambridge: LDA Learning

Selbst, M.C. and Gordon, S.B. (2012) *POWER-Solving® Stepping Stones to Solving Life's Everyday Social Problems*. Somerset, NJ: HI-STEP, LLC.

Timms, L.A. (2011) *60 Social Situations and Discussion Starters*. London: Jessica Kingsley Publishers.

Varughese, T. (2011) *Social Communication Cues for Young Children with Autism Spectrum Disorders and Related Conditions*. London: Jessica Kingsley Publishers.

Bullying and teasing

Dubin, N. (2006) *Being Bullied* (DVD). London: Jessica Kingsley Publishers.

Dubin, N. (2007) *Asperger Syndrome and Bullying: Strategies and Solutions*. London: Jessica Kingsley Publishers.

Gray, C. and Williams, J. (2006) *No Fishing Allowed: "Reel" In Bullying* (Manual and DVD). Arlington, TX: Future Horizons.

Heinrichs, R. (2003) *Perfect Targets: Asperger Syndrome and Bullying*. Shawnee Mission, KS: Autism Asperger Publishing Company.

Tickle, A. and Stott, B. (2010) *Exploring Bullying with Adults with Autism and Asperger Syndrome*. London: Jessica Kingsley Publishers.

Puberty and sexuality

Attwood, S. (2008) *Making Sense of Sex.* London: Jessica Kingsley Publishers.

Edmonds, G. and Beardon, L. (2008) *Asperger Syndrome and Social Relationships.* London: Jessica Kingsley Publishers.

Edmonds, G. and Worton, D. (2006) *The Asperger Personal Guide.* London: Sage Publications.

Hénault, I. (2006) *Asperger's Syndrome and Sexuality.* London: Jessica Kingsley Publishers.

Lawson, W. (2005) *Sex, Sexuality and the Autism Spectrum.* London: Jessica Kingsley Publishers.

Shockley, T. (2009) *The Love-Shy Survival Guide.* London: Jessica Kingsley Publishers.

Uhlenkamp, J. (2009) *The Guide to Dating for Teenagers with Asperger Syndrome.* Shawnee Mission, KS: Autism Asperger Publishing Company.

A MOTHER'S JOURNEY TO SAVE HER FAMILY

Kitty Dubin

I am a journal keeper and have been for most of my life. Writing in a journal every day helps me keep track of and process my life. I like to look back after a period of time and read what I have written to see what was going on and how I felt about it. On October 5, 2010, the day before the FBI raid on Nick's apartment, I had written in my journal, "This is the happiest time of my life." This expression of joy was not triggered by any particular event, like celebrating a birthday or taking a much-anticipated trip, but rather by a general feeling of hard-earned contentment.

Because of the myriad of problems Nick had growing up, my husband Larry and I had to constantly advocate for him. At school, on the playground, in the neighborhood—there was a continual succession of fires that needed to be put out and we were always on call. In addition, Nick was socially isolated from his peers, which meant we were his best friends by default. To say we were involved parents is a cosmic understatement. To say we were an enmeshed family would also be true.

This pattern of enmeshment didn't change significantly until after Nick was diagnosed with Asperger's syndrome at the age of twenty-seven. Finally, understanding why he was different for the first time in his life and identifying his career path all in the same day had been incredibly empowering for him. However, the biggest growth spurt in terms of his independence took place while he was in his doctoral program in psychology. During the five years he was pursuing that degree, he received excellent grades, took better care of himself and his living space, and developed his first close friendship with a classmate.

His career as an advocate for people with Asperger's was also taking off. He was writing books, producing DVDs, and traveling around the country giving presentations. His life was filled with activity and purpose. We no longer felt we had to be as involved with him and could let go of our role as micromanagers. For years, we had struggled to create a healthy separation with little success, and were now thrilled that it was finally happening.

After Nick was diagnosed, I read that an alarmingly high percentage of those with Asperger's are either unemployed or under employed. That was a devastating statistic and one that haunted me for years. What kind of employment would Nick ever be suited for? I knew he could not just take any job. It would have to be one that was genuinely fulfilling for him, but after failing to get his teaching certificate, and knowing he couldn't be a practicing psychologist because of the social limitations of his disability, I couldn't imagine what that would be.

My worries were over when, after receiving his doctoral degree, Nick was offered a position as a consultant to the faculty of a school for students with Asperger's. It was too good to be true. Not only would he be employed, but the job was in line with his goal of wanting to help others on the autism spectrum. Also, he was also getting good pay and excellent benefits. Larry and I could finally exhale.

The job seemed to be going very well. The headmaster told us how valuable Nick was to the school because of his vast knowledge of Asperger's and his ability to translate that information to the teachers. Larry and I began to plan some vacations. We felt more comfortable about going away for longer periods of time now that Nick's life was more settled and he didn't need our support as much anymore. I think we were all feeling liberated from the many struggles that had kept the three of us joined at the hip for so many years. A major shift was taking place and life was good. I was reflecting on all these positive changes the day I wrote in my journal, "This is the happiest time of my life."

The next morning the phone rang at nine thirty. I could see from the caller ID that it was Larry. Judging from the time, I figured he was probably on his way to work. Hearing the tone of his voice instantly alarmed me. It was not loud or hysterical. On the contrary, it was quiet and controlled. "Are you sitting down?" he asked. I said that I wasn't. I was standing in the kitchen drinking a cup of English breakfast tea. He told me I needed to sit down right away. Now, I was scared. Had Nick been in a car accident? Was Nick sick? What the hell was wrong? Again, his voice was intense, not much above a whisper. "It's all over," he said.

"What's all over?" I asked.

"Everything," he said.

In the blink of an eye, Nick had lost everything he had worked so hard for: his reputation, his job, his self-esteem, and his independence. Larry and I were instantly thrown back into our former roles as Nick's advocates, only this time, it was not because he was being bullied or had failed a test and needed an accommodation. He had been arrested for a federal offense and the rest of his life was at stake.

The trauma of Nick's arrest was so great that it was not possible for him to continue living at his apartment. He moved back home the same day. He was shaken to the core and so were we. We knew right away that our family needed to stay close together in order to deal with whatever was going to unfold even though we had no idea what that would be.

That morning our family entered a kind of portal into a world that we had only heard about but had never personally experienced: the criminal justice system. Even though Larry had been a practicing attorney early in his career, he was rarely involved in criminal defense work. And certainly none of us had ever been a defendant in a criminal case. We were like Alice in Wonderland falling down the rabbit hole. We had suddenly been transported into a world that was strange and frightening to us. It was a world without compassion; a world that was totally dehumanizing; and a world in which we had no control.

I couldn't believe that after nine years on his own, Nick was now living at home again. I wondered how we would ever adjust to these radically new circumstances. I know it's common these days for adult children to temporarily move back home until they get back on their feet financially, but this was a completely different situation. Nick's return to the nest did not feel temporary at all and it was unclear what it would take for him to ever get back on his feet.

After his arrest, the terror we all felt created an immediate collapse of the boundaries we had worked so hard to previously establish. For starters, Larry and I no longer had any privacy. We soon discovered we could not even have a private conversation unless Nick was asleep or away from the house. His Asperger's understandably amplified the fear and uncertainty of what could happen to him, so he needed to be physically close to us most of the time.

The three of us found ourselves quickly returning to old behaviors that had all but disappeared in recent years. Once again, I was nagging Nick to do his laundry and clean his room while Larry was constantly reminding him to exercise and watch his weight. Naturally, Nick resented being told what to do after living on his own for so long. It felt that in a week our family had regressed at least ten years. The day after his arrest, Nick was put on an ankle tether that monitored whether or not he was at home. For all intents and purposes, our family was put on an invisible tether that inextricably bound us together for the next two-and-a-half years. Because of the horrific nature of the situation into which we had been thrust, we lost all the ground we had previously gained and were once again a deeply enmeshed family.

An issue we had to confront almost immediately was whom to tell and whom not to tell about what had happened. We didn't want the stress of having to inform all our friends and family and then have the additional burden of keeping them updated. So initially we told only a handful of people. That decision was a double-edged sword. It made us (especially me) feel isolated, but it helped to conserve our energy and gave us a sense of security that only a few people were aware of this highly private and personal matter.

That sense of security was completely shattered ten days after Nick's arrest. We were shocked and horrified to learn there had been a local television news story about him, replete with misinformation, and it had gone viral on the internet. After that, other than those we had specifically told, there was no way to know which of our friends, relatives, neighbors, and co-workers were aware of what happened. It was a bizarre predicament to be in and created extreme discomfort and vulnerability whenever we ran into anyone we knew.

One night at a movie theater, Larry and I bumped into a couple with whom we used to socialize. We attempted to have a normal conversation with them but came away from the encounter with totally different reactions. I was convinced they didn't know and Larry was convinced they did. There was really no way to know for sure.

Our isolation was compounded by the uniqueness of our particular experience. We were grieving deeply, but it wasn't as if someone in our family was ill or had died. There were no support groups to join and no one sent sympathy cards or left casseroles at our front door. Even if friends knew what had transpired, many assumed, often incorrectly, that contacting us would be intrusive. I suspect that is a rationalization people often use to convince themselves they are doing the right thing, rather than having the courage to make what could be an uncomfortable phone call and not know what to say.

No one who knew Nick was ever judgmental because they intuitively sensed that what he had done was related to his lack of social development rather than any type of criminal behavior. Being judgmental was not the problem. The problem was that people did not know what to say in such unusual circumstances and wound up saying things that either hurt or infuriated me. Some friends tried their best to be sympathetic, but often said things that unintentionally made me feel worse. Here are a few of these comments I've selected from my journal: "I can't imagine anything worse ever happening to me." "I couldn't go on if I were you." "This too shall pass." "Why don't you and Larry go on a cruise, have some fun, and get away from all this?" "Do you think this will ruin Nick's life?"

I realize how difficult it was for others to put themselves in our shoes, especially because the situation was so far removed from anything they had personally experienced. That said, I don't believe anyone who is dealing with such painful circumstances wants to be pitied, told how awful their plight is, or offered a simplistic solution that diminishes their grief. I understand how challenging it is to come up with the right thing to say to someone who is in the depths of such despair. Every situation is different, but a few weeks after Nick's arrest, I received a blank note card from a friend with only one handwritten word on it: Courage. That spoke volumes.

For the first six months of this crisis, we had to live with the real possibility that Nick could be sent to prison. We knew he could not last a day if he were incarcerated and yet we had to cope with this haunting specter every day. Larry and I were scared to death, and Nick perseverated on it constantly because of his Asperger's. He was obsessed by the thought every waking moment and his anxiety became debilitating. He couldn't sleep or have a single moment of peace. He would pace, sweat profusely, and often have trouble simply breathing. Although we were all dealing with tremendous fear, Nick's Asperger's exacerbated his anxiety to a dangerously high level.

Our fear intensified at night when we were at our most exhausted and vulnerable. Nick talked repeatedly about not wanting to live any more. We did not know what to say or do to comfort him. There were times when we got so scared we thought we should take him to the hospital, but we were afraid that would only make matters worse. In our heart of hearts, Larry and I believed that his need to voice these dark feelings was more of an expression of wanting his pain to end than actually wanting to take his life. I truly understood how he felt. From time to time, I, too, was plagued with thoughts of not wanting to go on.

I am normally a very organized and focused person, but fear and anxiety were wreaking havoc on my daily life. I was constantly searching for my glasses, leaving papers at home that I needed for work, and burning food on the stove that I had completely forgotten about. The only time I could really concentrate on anything other than Nick's case was when I was teaching. This was my fourteenth year as a lecturer in playwriting at Oakland University. I have also been a playwright for the past thirty years and have had my work produced at theaters throughout the country. Playwriting is my passion and I love teaching the subject to others. When I walked into the classroom, somehow I was able to compartmentalize and leave everything else at home. Teaching a two-hour class was like going on a trip. I could temporarily put my troubles aside, be in the present moment, and feel like myself again. Teaching became my anchor and salvation for the next six semesters.

As strange as this may sound, I went to work the day after the arrest. I am not sure why, other than I had a strong need to stick to my routine. Driving to school that day, I wondered how I would manage to get through my two classes. What if I broke down and started to cry in front of my students? What if I couldn't put a sentence together? What if I had to be carried out on a stretcher? I was so distraught that I didn't remember we were discussing the play, *Doubt*, that day. *Doubt* is about a nun, who is the principal of a Catholic school and is convinced that a priest at her school has molested a student. The audience never finds out whether or not her suspicions are true. There is a particular sermon the priest delivers about gossip that we discussed that day. The point of the sermon is that once gossip destroys a person's reputation, it is like a pillow that has been taken outside and stabbed with a knife. The wind scatters the feathers everywhere, making it impossible for the pillow to ever be put back together again. The sermon made me think about Nick's hard-earned reputation and whether or not it would ever be restored.

The days I taught were much better than those I didn't. When I wasn't teaching, I had no structure and spent much of the time crying. I cried everywhere: in restaurants; in doctors' offices; in my car; in movie theaters; in the park; even in the library. My grief knew no bounds. I felt bad when Nick saw me cry and I made a concerted effort to leave the house if I felt a wave of sadness starting to come over me. I drove to a nearby lake, parked my car, and would start to sob, screaming at the top of my lungs, sometimes for as long as an hour. When I was all cried out, I then drove home, and tried to act "normal."

One day when I was feeling especially preoccupied, I blew through two stop signs without even realizing it. The wail of a police siren brought me back to reality and I was immediately pulled over. I don't know if it was the sound of the siren or having to deal with the law, but I started crying hysterically. Concerned about my mental state, the officer asked me if I was under a doctor's care. I had recently started seeing a psychiatrist because I was having trouble sleeping, so I nodded yes and continued to sob. He then made a call on his cell and within minutes, a chaplain from the police department arrived. The officer and the chaplain were clearly worried that I was having some kind of breakdown and kept asking me what was wrong. I couldn't speak and I couldn't stop crying. Chaplain Tim, as he told me to call him, talked to me for quite a while until I stopped crying, although to this day I don't remember a single word he said. Finally he gave me his card and the two men took off, like the Lone Ranger and Tonto, leaving me to collect myself and drive the three blocks home. Their compassion that day was a pinhole of light in an otherwise pitch-black scenario. The officer's kindness even extended to not giving me a ticket.

When I wasn't teaching or crying, Larry and I were actively involved in Nick's case. Our lawyers were not that familiar with

Asperger's and because we were, we helped them research forensic psychologists with a specialty in autism spectrum disorder (ASD) whom they might contact to evaluate Nick and determine what role, if any, his disability played in the offense he committed. We thought having someone of national repute would be important to the case and our lawyers thought it was equally important to have someone local. We discovered that, even in an area as large as Metropolitan Detroit, it was difficult to find a forensic psychologist who had expertise in ASDs.

We learned early on that our lawyers were excellent at doing their jobs, but were not there to provide psychological counseling or to hold our hands. In that respect, we were on our own, venturing into new and unexplored territory without having anyone to talk to who had been down this frightening road before. Our journey was like the *Life of Pi*. We felt alone in uncharted waters, traveling together in very close quarters, not knowing where we were going or how we were going to get there.

For the type of emotional and spiritual support we desperately needed, we turned to Julia Press, who has been our family counselor since 1997. She immediately came to our aid, making herself available to us from the day of the arrest right through to the present. Her advice was often simple to understand but very difficult to put into practice. "Stay in the present and take it one step at a time," she would tell me repeatedly. What she said made sense. The problem was I couldn't do it for more than three minutes at a time. If I thought about the future or started to anticipate what could happen next, it was like falling off a cliff into the abyss. I had to learn over time to become vigilant about my thoughts in order to maintain any kind of emotional equilibrium. Julia has been a lifeline to our family, especially to me. Without her daily calls of encouragement, wisdom, and steadfast love, I would not have been able to survive. Throughout this entire journey, she has never once let go of my hand.

After our lawyers submitted the first set of expert reports, we had to wait four months for a response from the prosecutor. It was like finding a lump in your breast and having a mammogram to find out if it's cancerous, but the doctor won't tell you when the results will be in, so day after day you sit by the phone waiting for his call. I can't describe the agony these tortuous and protracted waiting periods caused our family, especially because there was no explanation for why things were taking so long. This agony was doubly compounded for Nick whose nervous system can't tolerate uncertainty, especially of this magnitude. He would constantly verbalize his fears over and over again and literally not be able to think about anything else. He also did not have the distractions of teaching that Larry and I had, where we could temporarily put aside his worries and focus on other things.

We were living in a cauldron of tension and were so overwrought that we did what any family would probably do under similar circumstances. We took our anger and frustration out on each other. We couldn't get mad at the prosecutors or our lawyers, but these feelings had to come out somewhere and they frequently got displaced on each other. So, on top of all the suffering we were going through with the case, we were also inflicting pain on each other. To our credit, usually after we had one of these fights, we would have a family meeting to try to work out our differences and return to a place of love and caring.

We felt great relief when the prosecution finally responded by taking prison off the table. However, they said they were still confused about Asperger's syndrome and didn't understand how it differed from a mental or emotional illness. Our experts then wrote another detailed set of reports to answer that question, while we continued to wait in anguish.

Larry and I had celebrated our forty-first wedding anniversary the month before Nick's arrest. We were probably in the best place we had ever been. Over the years, we had gone through some marital therapy and learned how to resolve conflict in a way that precluded one of us having to be right and the other having to be wrong. It had taken a long time to get there, but we had developed a solid communication process and were each other's best friend. We enjoyed socializing with other couples, but when the weekend came, our favorite thing to do was spend that time together.

But grief, stress, exhaustion, and a child in severe emotional pain take a tremendous toll on a marriage and our relationship began to deteriorate under the huge strain of this ordeal. Fights would constantly erupt. We were both emotionally raw and something as small as an eye roll or a shift in tone could trigger a huge confrontation. A major source of conflict between us was that I frequently wanted Larry to contact our lawyers to find out why things were taking so long. He would refuse and then my level of anger would jump from one to a hundred in a matter of seconds. One night I got into such a fit of rage towards him, I tripped and fell on the bathroom floor, breaking my toe and little finger. That was a wakeup call that my anger had become totally out of control.

The real problem underlying all this tension and volatility was that neither of us had anything left to give. Our tanks were on empty. We were both exhausted from maintaining our teaching jobs, tending to Nick's intense emotional needs, working on the case, and dealing with the constant fear and uncertainty of how this would all end. We were usually in a stupor by seven o'clock every night. We each wanted to be loved and appreciated, but the truth was that we were both completely depleted. It wasn't until we could see beyond our own pain and truly empathize with each other, that we were able to find our footing again.

By far the most difficult emotional aspect of this entire experience has been watching Nick suffer and not being able to do anything about it. I love my son with all my heart and seeing him so traumatized on a daily basis has been gut wrenching for me. Like any parent, I wanted to fix it, make it better, or at least, be able to comfort him. As a mother, it has been excruciating not to be able to protect him from the horrors and indignities to which he has been subjected. Nick is a kind and gentle soul, and seeing him be treated like a criminal has broken my heart a million times a day.

Of course this wasn't the first time Larry and I weren't able to protect him. We couldn't protect him from being bullied; we couldn't protect him from failing at student teaching; and we couldn't protect him from getting type 2 diabetes. But now those situations seemed inconsequential in comparison to the potential realities of being a lifelong felon and a registered sex offender.

Aside from the emotional stress it was causing me, watching Nick suffer and being powerless to do anything about it was also making me physically sick. During this time, I developed shingles, insomnia, and a gastrointestinal problem that caused me to lose ten pounds in three months (my normal weight is one hundred pounds). I realized that if I were going to survive, I needed to separate myself more from Nick, both physically and emotionally. That may sound callous, but let me explain.

Most mothers (and fathers for that matter) would readily admit that when their child is in pain, they are in pain. No matter how young or how old, our children are always our babies. We feel a responsibility to protect them and that sense of responsibility is greatly magnified with a child who has a disability.

That was my dilemma. When Nick was in despair, I was in despair. This transfer of emotions was automatic and happened so quickly there was seemingly nothing I could do about it. Larry, who loves Nick every bit as much as I do, did not have this problem to the same degree. He was able to separate himself more from Nick's pain and not allow it to drag him under.

I felt bad for Larry because when I fell apart, then he would have two very depressed people to deal with, instead of one. I also knew that it didn't do Nick any good to see me constantly crying or lying in bed like a zombie. So for Larry's and Nick's sakes as well as mine, I knew I had to find some way to become less affected by Nick's pain, but I had no idea how to do so. In some strange way, I felt I would be abandoning Nick if I weren't suffering right along with him. I seemed to embody the belief, "You can only be as happy as your least happy child."

I turned to Julia for help with this terrible conundrum. She made the analogy to being on a plane that is in distress. The flight attendant announces that when the oxygen masks come down, parents should place them over their faces first or they won't be able to help their children. Suddenly, I got it. Unless I took care of myself first, I would be of no use to Nick. When I began to accept the truth of that logic, I knew I had to figure out ways to take better care of myself. But first I had to convince myself that doing so did not mean I was abandoning Nick.

This was difficult to do at first, but not because of anything Nick did or said. He never tried to discourage me from going out. I just felt this tremendous guilt. How could I go and enjoy a movie while he was home in so much pain? I gradually started making plans with friends once a week to go out to eat or see a movie or a play. I went to Chicago with a friend for the weekend, which, after two years of not being away, even overnight, felt like going to Hawaii for a month. Finally, I began to swim in my own lane instead of swimming in Nick's. Larry and I also decided to go to a local hotel to spend the night. I had to push myself really hard to do these things, but once I did them, I felt somewhat better and was more able to support Nick and Larry.

In spite of these occasional outings, we had little to no relief from the constant feeling of dread that enveloped us like a thick fog. Our lives had become the horror version of the film *Groundhog*

Day, with each day being much like the one that preceded it. One of the pleasures Larry and I missed the most was traveling. Being creatures of habit, we had vacationed at the same places every year but never tired of them: Vermont in the summer, Florida over Christmas break, New York in the spring, and Cleveland, my hometown, for the Thanksgiving holiday. For three years in a row, we had not gone to any of these places or anywhere else for that matter. Our home had become a virtual prison.

People kept asking us why we didn't leave all the stress behind and just get away for a few days. Here's why. By law, Nick was not permitted to leave Southeastern Michigan while he was on the tether. Although there was nothing legally stopping Larry and me from leaving town, we knew we wouldn't be able to enjoy ourselves, even for a couple of days, with Nick at home in such a highly vulnerable state.

When I look back on the duration of Nick's case, the image of a prizefight comes to mind. In round one, Larry, Nick, and I entered the ring scared but optimistic, based on our lawyers' belief that Nick had a very strong case. As we went through the early rounds and prison was taken off the table, we felt a surge of hope as well as some concern because the prosecution still didn't understand how Asperger's differed from an emotional or mental illness.

The "fight" went on much longer than expected and in the later rounds, we began to lose steam—physically, mentally, and emotionally. We received a major blow when Nick was evaluated by the FBI psychologist in Washington DC who agreed with all our experts, but for some unexplained reason, the prosecutor ignored his own expert's opinion.

Months passed and, like a fighter struggling to get back on his feet after a series of major blows, the prosecution hit us again even harder. They wanted Nick to be examined by yet another forensic psychologist, bringing the total number of evaluations to five. This latest was someone who had no expertise in Asperger's, which was alarming. Larry and I felt horrible about Nick being put through another grueling examination but we felt we had no choice. It was our last shred of hope.

We had to wait four months (with no explanation why) before this evaluation was even scheduled. It was another unbearably long waiting period that really took all of us to the brink of sanity. A month after the evaluation was completed, we were sent a copy of the report and were ecstatic to read that the examiner used language that supported the other experts' favorable disposition about Nick. However, knowing how things had gone in the past, we felt anything but confident.

After living in this hellish limbo for two-and-a-half years, I was at the point where I just wanted the whole nightmare to be over. I soon got my wish. Ken, our lawyer, said the prosecutors were meeting to render a final decision in Nick's case and he would call us immediately with their decision. The three of us sat by the phone and waited, our hearts beating as one. The phone rang. Larry saw the caller ID and said, "It's Ken." We held our collective breath. Larry picked up the phone. I didn't even have to hear what Ken was saying. The expression on Larry's face said it all. It was the final knock-out punch.

Once again, we were crushed, but at last, our long and tortured battle with the federal government was over. That brought a small measure of relief. One chapter had ended and a new one would soon begin. This new one will undoubtedly present daunting challenges, but hopefully not as overwhelming as the ones we have already faced. Having been stuck in the same place for so long, we are eager to move forward with our lives. The following are some of the goals we have set for ourselves in an effort to do so.

As a family, we will have to start from scratch to once again create a healthy separation. This will be extremely hard to accomplish because of how inseparable we have become, both emotionally and physically, for such a long period of time. Nick plans to move out of our house and into his own place, which will help facilitate the separation process. Nick's move to live alone is daunting for him in so many ways.

Each of us will also have to come to terms with what we believe to be a terrible injustice. Eckhart Tolle, the well-known and respected spiritual teacher, has said that in order to find inner peace, it is often necessary to "accept the unacceptable." Of course, in practical terms, we have to accept the reality of Nick's sentence with all its many and terrible restrictions, but we do not have to accept the unfairness of it.

The unduly harsh sentence that Nick has received will exponentially increase the number of challenges he faces in trying to put his life back together. Being a lifelong felon and a registered sex offender would be difficult for anyone to adjust to, but for someone on the autism spectrum who has so many other obstacles to deal with in life, these punishments seem cruel and unnecessary. For example, the incredibly complex restrictions of the registry make traveling, even for a few days, a complicated bureaucratic nightmare. But far worse than these physical restrictions are the shame and fear Nick will have to cope with in being labeled a sex offender by the federal government.

There is no question that these goals will be profoundly challenging for our family to pursue and will require time, perseverance, and courage. Recently, I heard the sister of one of the Boston Marathon victims talking on the news about what her brother has gone through in losing his leg. In describing his attitude, she said, "You don't know how strong you are until being strong is the only choice you have left." That statement really resonated with me. Throughout this experience, I have become more resilient. Over and over again, I continue to dig deeper and deeper to find the will to survive. As individuals, and as a family, Larry, Nick, and I have all discovered reserves of strength we never knew we had, which I hope will serve us in the coming months and years as we try to move forward and rebuild our lives.

Before closing my chapter, I would like to respond to a question I suspect many readers might be asking themselves: why in the world would a mother allow her son to share such an incredibly personal story in such a public way? Here is my answer.

Like many who suffer through a tragedy, I want this experience to count for something. I want to take what we have learned from this painful ordeal and have others benefit from our hard-earned knowledge.

Three months after Nick was diagnosed with AS, Larry and Nick decided to produce a DVD called *Diagnosis Asperger's: Nick Dubin's Journey of Self-discovery*. Their goal in making this DVD was to educate others about AS by putting a human face to the condition. When they told me about their idea, I was dead set against it. I was afraid of what the public's reaction might be. Wisely, Nick and Larry ignored my fears and made the DVD. It turned out to be the first of many contributions Nick has made to the autism community where he shared his personal experiences in an effort to help others. In a way, this book is an extension and a continuation of that path he so bravely began to walk ten years ago.

The decision to write this book has been an epic struggle for our family. It represents a clash of values that we hold very dear. As parents, we want to protect Nick from any negativity that is bound to result from bringing forth such a sensitive subject. At the same time, we believe that not sharing this information would be almost criminal. It would be like knowingly allowing someone to walk across a field where mines were planted and not warning him of the possibility of stepping on one. Wrestling with this conflict of values has been agonizing for us and we have had to re-make this decision many times over. Ultimately, we came to the conclusion that keeping this information to ourselves would not only be selfish but it would be morally wrong. The Talmud, a central text of Rabbinic Judaism, states, "If you can save one life it is as if you have saved the entire world." We may never know if that goal will be achieved, but for now, the hope of achieving it will have to suffice.

A FATHER'S JOURNEY TO PROTECT HIS SON
A LEGAL PERSPECTIVE

Larry Dubin

Introduction

On October 6, 2010, the morning started out in a typically routine manner only to become the worst day of my life. I left my home in suburban Detroit to drive downtown to work. It was a beautiful, sunny fall day. Life seemed good. I was on my way to the University of Detroit Mercy School of Law, where I have been a law professor for the past thirty-five years and taught classes in legal ethics, evidence, trial practice, and advanced seminars. I loved teaching law students how they can use their skills to make a positive contribution to society. I was an ardent believer in the legal system and very proud to be a lawyer.

My positive attitude about being a lawyer came from having practiced law for almost a decade, following my graduation from the University of Michigan Law School, before starting my academic career in 1975. During my years practicing law, I litigated many different kinds of cases, representing all kinds of clients, from wealthy corporate executives to indigent clients. I have had numerous articles and several books published about legal ethics, rules of evidence, and effective techniques for trial lawyers. For eight years I served as a member of the Michigan Attorney Grievance Commission (appointed by the Michigan Supreme Court), which has the responsibility to investigate and prosecute lawyers who commit acts of misconduct. I have also received multiple awards from the State Bar of Michigan for public television documentaries that I have produced to help people better understand and appreciate the workings of our legal system. In my programs, I strove to illustrate how injustices could be rectified by the legal system. As a documentarian, I had the honor of interviewing Rosa Parks, her famous civil rights attorney Fred Gray, the late United States congresswoman Barbara Jordan, and others whom I greatly admire for being fighters for justice.

On my way to the law school that fateful morning, I received a call on my cell phone. An unfamiliar voice identified himself as an FBI agent. I immediately assumed the call had something to do with a former student who needed a recommendation for a job in government. I had frequently received calls from the FBI for that purpose. However, this call was different and turned out to be a life-changing moment. The male voice told me he was in the process of executing a search warrant at my son Nick's apartment concerning his personal computer. I learned later that child pornography was found on his computer. The agent thought that it would be wise for me to come there immediately due to Nick's emotional and physical condition. When I arrived at Nick's apartment, there were close to a dozen FBI agents milling around both inside and outside of his small quarters. Nick was on his couch in a fetal position with half his face tucked under a pillow. I went over to him, and in front of the agents who were present, put my arm around him and whispered in his ear, "I love you."

Statement of full disclosure

As a lawyer and Nick's father, I recognize that some readers may discount my statements as being biased. Although I admit that I love Nick with all my heart, I would never rationalize or not take seriously any criminal act that would knowingly and directly harm a child. My intention in this chapter is to share my personal experience in helping Nick cope with the criminal justice system, as well as to impart the research I've gathered during this process. I do not believe that those on the autism spectrum are more likely to be criminals or child predators. In fact, I believe just the opposite. People on the autism spectrum tend to be honest, law-abiding individuals. I also want to be clear that as a lawyer, I understand the importance of stating the facts of a case in an honest manner. In Nick's case, the facts were never substantially in dispute. What was in dispute was the appropriate way to resolve his case.

As difficult and challenging as life has been for Nick, I have always marveled at his resiliency. Throughout his life, he has had to cope with many barriers and obstacles as well as his neurological limitations. As a result of these difficulties, he has suffered from chronic depression and anxiety. Nevertheless, Nick has always had the courage to confront these challenges and to maximize his potential while trying to help others avoid or successfully cope with some of the same hardships that he experienced.

Sexual exploration v. sex offender

Nick is the last person anyone would have imagined becoming involved in the criminal justice system. He has never acted in an aggressive way towards anyone and prefers solitude to socializing. Others might perceive him as quirky or different, but no one ever has a bad word to say about him. He is simply a kind and gentle soul, or as one expert stated, just, "a good person."

Throughout Nick's life, my wife and I have tried to provide him with the necessary emotional support he needed as a result of his lack of social interaction with peers. When he was bullied at school or had academic problems, we would do whatever we could to try to alleviate the problem. We frequently met with his teachers, who didn't seem to understand his academic needs and often wrote him off as not trying hard enough, which was not the case. Every week or so, another problem would pop up that required our intervention and support.

Children on the autism spectrum tend to be very dependent on their parents and have many needs that can be extremely challenging for parents to meet. This point is well stated in Andrew Solomon's (2012) acclaimed book, *Far From the Tree*. In referencing the disability of autism, he states (p.6): "If you have a child with a disability, you are forever the parent of a disabled child; it is one of the primary facts about you, fundamental to the way other people perceive you." In other words, you are never free from feeling a sense of responsibility for the wellbeing of your child even as he or she ages through adulthood.

Nick has written honestly about the difficulties he had socializing during his middle and high school years when he wasn't able to engage in the normal friendships or experiences of adolescence, like attending football games, school dances, or parties. Without normal social maturation, Nick experienced sexual identity issues that were beyond my understanding and required professional assistance. Like most parents, I wanted my child to be well liked and accepted by his peers. I wanted him to have friends who would always be welcome at our home. It was deeply painful for me to see Nick suffering as he realized that he didn't fit in with others and that he felt inferior to his peers, who seemed to enjoy being with each other. With the passing of every year, I hoped that Nick would mature a little more and become able to develop friendships with others. Yet in reality, as he became older it only became more difficult and painful for him to develop friendships with his peers. The gap between his intellectual growth and his social immobilization kept widening as time went on. By middle school and then into high school, he became very depressed and isolated. Being the victim of severe bullying and sexual taunting further intensified his dark moods and, as I subsequently learned, contributed to his sexual confusion. I was not aware at the time that he was being sexually harassed. What made matters even worse was that we had no idea what was causing his social adjustment problems as he had not been diagnosed at this time.

During his adolescence it was difficult for me to see Nick as a sexual person. He didn't socialize and never expressed any sexual interest in either males or females. It was obvious that he was lonely and in pain. More than anything, I just wanted him to be happy. To that end, I would take him on trips to spend time with him away from home. We would attend national tennis tournaments, visit and explore different cities, and go on adventures like whitewater rafting or hiking. My real intent on these ventures was to try to lift his spirits by giving him some breathing room through a change of environment. On these occasions, I would try to engage him in more open conversation about his feelings and inject some words of encouragement.

What I have come to realize is that Nick was and is a sexual being. Although that statement may seem obvious, many people on the autism spectrum are often viewed as asexual when in reality they simply have no sexual outlets. Raising a special needs child requires parents to address so many other problems that dealing with the issue of sexuality can easily take a back seat to the more pressing concerns that often arise on a daily basis.

Even under the best of circumstances, sex is never an easy subject for parents to discuss with their children. Through no fault of their own, children on the autism spectrum often lack the social skills necessary to develop into healthy sexual beings during the adolescent years. This lag in Nick's development was a major factor in bringing him into contact with the criminal justice system. Sadly, prosecutors often lack sufficient knowledge about people on the autism spectrum and misinterpret behavior that reflects sexual immaturity rather than the perpetration of a serious criminal act. I would never want to imply that people on the autism spectrum would likely commit a criminal act involving inappropriate sexual conduct. That would be like saying everyone with autism is a gifted pianist, a brilliant mathematician, or a talented painter, even though those talents might be causally related to being on the autism spectrum. I want to be clear that I am not making any generalizations about people on the autism spectrum. Rather, I hope that sharing Nick's story as well as the research I've uncovered will in some way resonate and be helpful to others.

The truth is Nick's viewing child pornography had nothing to do with ever wanting to hurt anyone, but rather reflected his delayed social and sexual development. What was an inappropriate and ill-advised way for Nick to gain more knowledge about sex through the use of his computer unwittingly resulted in a federal crime.

Bestselling author, John Elder Robison, discusses developmental delays in his article "Autism and porn: a problem no one talks about" (2013) in *Psychology Today*:

> Many people with autism experience significant developmental delays, and those delays are often imbalanced and even offset by exceptionalities in other areas. For example, when I was twelve, I had the language skills of a college professor with the social intelligence of a five-year-old... Harmless as that was, it shows the disparity between emotional and logical development that can exist in a person with autism.

The challenge I faced after Nick's arrest was to help Nick's lawyers find the most knowledgeable experts to offer their honest opinions to the prosecutors as to what the most appropriate and reasonable disposition should be for the charges brought against him. I knew I had to do some research to better understand how to proceed.

Since his diagnosis in 2004, I had put a lot of effort into educating myself on autism spectrum disorders (ASDs). I attended many autism meetings and had even been a speaker at a national conference. During that time I had never heard or read any information about autism and sexual development issues. However, after Nick's arrest, what I learned from my research shocked and compelled me to make this information available to those on the autism spectrum, their parents, mental health professionals, and those in the legal system.

Autism, sexuality, and the law: a hidden issue

The first piece of information I came across in my research took my breath away. It was a detailed letter written on August 4, 2008, two years before Nick's arrest, by Ami Klin, Ph.D. who, at the time, was the Harris Professor of Child Psychology and Psychiatry at the Yale University Child Study Center and is presently Professor and Division Chief of Autism and Related Disorders at Emory University School of Medicine. Dr Klin's letter had been sent to a federal judge as well as to the prosecuting attorney and defense lawyer in a case where an Asperger's defendant was to be sentenced for the crime of possession of child pornography. As one of the nation's leading experts on ASDs, Dr Klin (August 4, 2008) wrote that he had consulted with a number of individuals with Asperger's who faced the same charge, which "convinced me I was seeing the tip of the iceberg and, indeed, I have since learned that similar cases are beginning to arise in courtrooms around the country." Dr Klin expressed his fear that because those in the criminal justice system are unfamiliar with people on the autism spectrum, their behavior is "easy to misinterpret with devastating consequences." He emphatically stated, "This is an issue of national concern, which I and my colleagues feel compelled to begin to address through a systemic effort to educate stakeholders in the criminal justice system."

I was stunned that one of the leading experts about ASDs in the country was expressing this level of concern. I read Dr Klin's letter shortly after Nick's arrest and was afraid that those in the criminal justice system would not understand someone with Asperger's like

Nick. Dr Klin's letter was extremely illuminating in explaining why those with autism are especially vulnerable to viewing child pornography. I will be referring to his letter throughout my chapter.

I also discovered a report entitled *Joint Study Committee on Autism Spectrum Disorders and Public Safety* that was presented to the North Carolina General Assembly (2008). The legislature authorized the University of North Carolina School of Government, in consultation with the Autism Society of North Carolina and other organizations, to study and provide training to those in the legal system who deal with persons with autism. At that time, a document entitled *Autism Principles for Prosecutors* was released. This document, drafted by Michael D. Parker (2008), a North Carolina District Attorney, stated, "Prosecutors should take the nature and effects of autism spectrum disorder (ASD) into account in determining both whether to prosecute and how to resolve a criminal case involving a defendant affected by ASD." The study encouraged prosecutors to seek out ASD experts to help them in "evaluating appropriateness of such cases for prosecution." As for the specific crime of possession of child pornography, the recommendation was:

> Prosecutors should encourage therapeutic intervention… and seriously consider probationary periods and deferred prosecutions to monitor compliance before actual prosecutions in such cases… Prosecutors should pay particular attention to whether the offender has ASD, and whether there is any prior history of directly offending against children.

A separate and independently drafted document entitled, *Principles for Prosecutors Considering Child Pornography Charges Against Persons with Asperger's Syndrome* (Carley *et al.*, 2008) was sponsored by Dr Fred Volkmar, Director of the Child Study Center at Yale University and Professor of Pediatrics, of Psychiatry, and of Psychology and Chief of Child Psychiatry at Yale-New Haven Children's Hospital, along with major autism organizations, including Organization for Autism Research, Connecticut Autism Spectrum Resource Center, the Global and Regional Asperger Syndrome Partnership, MAAP Services for Autism and Asperger Syndrome, Asperger's Association of New England, and Asperger Syndrome and High Functioning Autism Association. This document stated that it was generated because, "enough cases have arisen to demonstrate the need for prosecutors to inform themselves of the condition and adopt a policy of restraint in the investigation and prosecution of such cases." The *Principles for Prosecutors* document puts forth the very same concerns expressed by Dr Ami Klin as well as the North Carolina Study:

> Given the lack of social adaption on the part of AS patients, interest in pornography as a means to explore ideas of sexuality…is expected. At these times AS is directly involved in the individual's obliviousness to the social and legal taboos surrounding child pornography and the inability to intuit that the visual depictions are the product of any kind of abusive relationships. This behavior is not predictive of future involvement with child pornography or offenses against children. There is nothing inherent in Autism Spectrum Disorders to make individuals inclined to sexual deviance of any kind… Persons with AS are far less likely to be predators than victims, because of their naiveté and ineptness in interpreting or deflecting the advances of others and their inability to initiate social contact with others or effectively direct or manipulate any social contact. (pp. 1–2)

The document goes on to discuss the need for not pursuing criminal prosecution in these cases:

> Asperger's Syndrome is a lifelong disability which on its own creates substantial hurdles for the patient. Criminal prosecution, conviction and the typical sanctions imposed in such cases are not necessary to protect the public in the case of an AS patient, but they are imponderably harsh, cruel and debilitating to persons with AS and their families on whom they are dependent. Generally these individuals are not a threat to society: it's the other way around. AS patients are frequently the target of abuses… (p.2)

Along with these documents, I came across a recent study that found that adolescents with ASDs are clearly vulnerable to being criminally charged as sex offenders (Fenclau *et al.*, 2012). This study examined thirty-seven male juveniles who had been charged with some type of sexual offense and were evaluated to determine whether any of them were on the autism spectrum. The findings showed that twenty-two of the thirty-seven defendants (60%) were diagnosed to be on the spectrum. Fenclau *et al.* (2012, p.8) concluded, "Given the current findings showing the presence of individuals with ASD in the sex offender population, it is clear that the acquisition of sexual knowledge and development of individuals with ASD should be further examined."

My research also included an article by Natalie Gougeon (2010) that explored the sexual development and conduct of autistic people. Gougeon recognized that ASD individuals are sexual beings who have difficulties in their sexual development due to their social disability. She states (p.354), "While individuals with autism do present with development delays in many areas, their physical development is not equally delayed." This finding certainly applied to Nick. As he got older, his physical development matured like others his age, yet his social and sexual development did not.

Besides the gap between physical and social/sexual development, there is also a divide between intellectual and social/sexual development. This was also true of Nick. He could easily write and deliver a two-hour presentation, but was too uncomfortable to socialize with the organizers afterwards. In high school he was captain of his tennis team but never fraternized with any of his teammates. Dr Klin comments on this gap (August 4, 2008):

> Asperger Syndrome is a disability of social cognition, social learning and communication... Adults, even those with high measured intelligence, may in a practical sense function like much younger children both emotionally and in their adaptive (life skills) behavior. Expectations for their understanding, skills and abilities are misplaced if development is based on IQ and chronological age.

Some other information I learned came unbidden to me. Over the past three years, I have received numerous calls from distraught parents who were referred to me by Dr Fred Volkmar as well as the Asperger's Association of New England. These parents contacted me because their adult sons had Asperger's and had been arrested for possession of child pornography. Although each case was different, the similarities were striking. These young men, who were all intelligent and in their twenties and thirties, had been socially isolated their entire lives and had no sexual experience. In none of these cases, as was true for Nick, was there concern that any of these individuals had inappropriate sexual contact with children. These parents told me their sons were not aware of the legal consequences of viewing child pornography or that they had even committed a crime. Talking to all these desperate parents made me extremely sad and also increased my awareness that Nick's was not an isolated case. In addition, I did some legal research and found many reported cases in both federal and state courts involving males on the autism spectrum charged with possession of child pornography. In these cases I read forensic psychological reports that were similar to the ones written about Nick.

Some of the parents with whom I spoke had sons who were currently serving time in prison and unable to cope with incarceration. I received one call from a woman whose nephew had been sent to federal prison for possession of child pornography. He could not deal with the harsh complexities of prison and eventually had to be put in solitary confinement where his life became unbearable. In his letter (August 4, 2008), Dr Klin wrote: "It is frankly, horrifying to contemplate what would happen to someone with this disability in a penal institution."

Dennis Debbault, Gary Mesibov Ph.D., and former judge Kimberly Taylor in their article, "Asperger syndrome in the criminal justice system" (2009), stated:

> People with AS often get into trouble without even realizing they have committed an offense. Offenses such as…child pornography and stalking…would certainly strike most of society as offenses that demand some sort of punishment. This assumption…may not take into account the particular issues that challenge an AS individual.

John Elder Robison also states in the previously quoted article that autistic defendants who are charged in sex crime cases "needed help much more help than punishment. Ignoring that reality is like ignoring the teachers who locked autistic people in basements at school when I was a kid."

In light of all the new information I was acquiring, I wasn't surprised to learn of the serious concern that Asperger's/autism organizations and leading mental health practitioners had about autistic defendants within the criminal justice system. These organizations and professionals are rightly worried about the harsh prosecutions and lengthy prison terms people on the autism spectrum who are convicted of possession of child pornography frequently receive.

To be completely clear, I have great sympathy for children who have been victimized by the production and distribution of their images in child pornography. I am an ardent proponent of the legal system ensuring and protecting the safety and the best interests of children. I strongly believe that adults who are child predators need to be severely punished. When children are endangered in any way, those who perpetrate these acts need to be vigorously prosecuted through the criminal justice system. At the same time, I also believe that people on the autism spectrum should not be unnecessarily prosecuted for behavior that is clearly related to their disability and does not pose any threat or danger to others. In these cases, compassion coupled with an appropriate treatment plan to rehabilitate and educate the person should be considered as a preferable alternative to a felony conviction with the possibility of prison and registration as a sex offender.

From the moment Nick was charged with this crime, I wanted to protect him from the severe consequences of the criminal justice system. The charges brought against him could result in a prison sentence as long as ten years. That realization was surreal and frightening beyond words. Nick has described in detail the FBI search of his apartment and his subsequent arraignment. In both instances, there was nothing I could do to protect my child (as I was frequently used to doing) other than to hire an attorney. It was not as if he was failing math, and I needed to hire a tutor, or go to his school to complain about him being bullied. The power of the federal government is massive. The fact that I could not protect Nick from the ongoing terror he was experiencing is a source of great sorrow and frustration for me.

Nick was fortunate to have lawyers who recognized the importance of him being evaluated by the most credible experts who would be in a position to educate the prosecutors about how his deficits may have contributed to the acts that brought him into the criminal justice system. For Nick, looking at adult and child pornography was a safe and solitary way to learn about his own sexuality. Because of his social disability, he was unable to acquire that experience through direct social contact with other people. Nick's use of his computer was the way he customarily acquired information about the outside world. The computer was like his auxiliary brain. Dr Klin (August 4, 2008) elaborates on this notion:

The Internet can be explored from the apparent security and privacy of one's own room. Most individuals with Aspergers Syndrome are very socially isolated. Curious about sex, it is not surprising that a person with Aspergers Syndrome would explore the abundant supply of erotic material freely available on the Internet. The problem arises, of course, because the material that is available on the Internet—and which is designed to attract attention and encourage interest—includes unlawful depictions of underage children.

Dr Klin's statements help clarify why the conduct Nick was charged with, was, in essence, a reflection of his private thoughts while using his computer as a safe way to learn about a part of his life that was not accessible to him. However, it makes sense that prosecutors would have difficulty understanding how someone like Nick with advanced college degrees could also be so naive. It would be confusing that someone could have such intellectual strengths and at the same time such serious social impairments. Without a clear explanation of asynchronous (uneven) development, prosecutors and judges would have difficulty understanding those on the autism spectrum.

After the FBI searched Nick's apartment, it took twenty-six months for the prosecution to formally charge him with one count of possession of child pornography. The reason for this long delay was that the prosecutors saw Nick as presenting a special case. Rather than immediately putting Nick's case on the trial docket, they were willing to review relevant information about Nick in deciding whether or not to prosecute him. This type of review, termed prosecutorial discretion, reflects the fact that not every person charged with a crime needs to or should be prosecuted. Nick's lawyers believed that through the use of this discretion, the prosecutors should place Nick in a diversion program. This option would have permitted Nick to meet the terms of a probationary period and receive the necessary rehabilitation, and at the end of that period, he would not have any criminal record.

As Nick described in his account, five different experts, two of them selected by the prosecution, evaluated him. Each of these experts intensively questioned Nick about his most private sexual thoughts. I would like to share some of their most important findings and opinions since this was the information that was made available to the prosecutors to make their final determination as to Nick's fate.

The defense experts

The first expert the defense lawyers consulted was the psychologist Nick had been regularly seeing for almost nine years. Dr Green is a highly regarded clinical psychologist who specializes in human sexuality. He stated in the conclusion of his report:

> Having worked closely with this young man over the last nine years, I can say in complete honesty that he is not only a very decent human being, but in light of his considerable impairment, a true innocent. I hope the prosecution can exercise not only the compassion but also the courage to spare this young man not only incarceration but the further inordinate burdens that would go along with a felony conviction.

Nick was also examined and tested by Dr Andrew Maltz, a highly respected forensic psychologist who specializes in ASDs. In his report to the prosecutors, he stated:

> Mr Dubin has never been aggressive towards others. He has never, prior to the aforementioned Complaint, been in trouble with the law. He has been vulnerable to others because of his inability to appreciate intent, and, to that end, he was exploited by his peer group as either an object of aggression or entertainment.

Dr Maltz also commented on the results of his extensive psychological testing of Nick:

> He does not have a personality profile, in any way that is consistent for individuals who are antisocial or psychopathic. His profile is not characteristic for individuals who will manipulate others, take advantage of others or lack a conscience regarding their behaviors... Mr Dubin does not think of children as sexual objects in a manner consistent for an adult with sexual drives who have, for unfortunate reasons, attached their interests to young children. It is highly unlikely for him to intentionally or purposefully plan or engage in bringing harm to anyone.

The third expert to examine Nick was Dr Fred Volkmar of Yale University. Nick met with Dr Volkmar who, after taking an extensive history and reading all relevant prior records, opined that a criminal conviction would be inappropriate. Dr Volkmar determined that Nick, even with above average intellectual skills, has, as a result of his neurological disability, severely delayed social skills and impaired real life (adaptive) skills. He states in his report: "Individuals with Asperger's disorder and autism have problems with social understanding, social learning and communication." He did not believe that Nick belonged in the criminal justice system, but would do well with properly administered therapy. He explained why Nick should receive appropriate psychological treatment as opposed to criminal prosecution:

> Most individuals with these conditions are victims rather than victimizers. The experience of bullying and social isolation is frequent. The sometimes rigid pursuit of collecting things often appears to mask or attempt to cope with chronic anxiety... It can take the form of interests in other kinds of inappropriate topics that can also cause legal difficulties. Fortunately, individuals with these conditions can respond to clear limit setting and a neuropsychologically informed psychotherapy where explicit guidance is provided. Nicolas appears both highly suited to such an approach and motivated to engage in it.

The extensive reports from these three highly qualified experts, as well as the FBI's analysis of the content on Nick's computer were submitted to the prosecutors. Based upon this information, prosecutors offered Nick an agreement to plead guilty to one count of possession of child pornography and probation. However, this agreement would cause Nick to have a lifelong felony conviction and registration as a sex offender. Nick's lawyers believed that this plea offer was not appropriate and in conflict with the recommendations from the experts that he be placed on diversion, receive therapy, and have no criminal record.

When that offer was refused, the prosecutors then informed Nick's lawyers that they didn't really understand how Asperger's differed from a mental illness. Nick's lawyers agreed to provide additional information to help the prosecutors understand that difference. Drs Green and Maltz wrote supplementary reports that explained in very clear terms how Asperger's, unlike a mental illness, is a pervasive neurological and developmental disorder that begins at birth and causes a widening gap over time between a person's intellectual capacity and his emotional, social, and sexual development. They also detailed how being on the autism spectrum impacted Nick's social and sexual development. When these supplemental reports were presented to the prosecutors, their contents were never disputed. However, the prosecutors still refused to change their plea offer to Nick requiring him to be a felon and a registered sex offender.

The prosecution experts

Nick's lawyers were very confident in the integrity and credibility of the experts who had examined Nick and their resulting opinions and recommendations. Yet when Nick's lawyers asked the prosecutors whether any of their experts had reviewed the reports, the prosecutors admitted that these reports had not been so examined. Nick's lawyers encouraged the prosecutors to therefore select their own expert to review the previously submitted reports. A month later, the prosecutors contacted Nick's lawyers and requested that Nick travel to the J. Edgar Hoover Building FBI headquarters in Washington DC to be examined by an FBI neuropsychologist who specialized in ASDs. As Nick mentioned earlier, this neuropsychologist worked for the FBI as Clinical Program Manager for the Office for Victim Assistance. In other words, he supervised the programs that offered assistance to children who were the victims of child pornography. The prosecutors informed Nick's lawyer at that time that this examination would provide the last information they would need in order to make a decision on the disposition of Nick's case.

Nick's lawyers believed that this offer was a positive sign that the prosecutors were trying to understand the special circumstances of this case. Consequently, a month later, Nick and I flew to Washington DC where he submitted to an intensive four-hour examination with the FBI neuropsychologist who had reviewed all the previously submitted reports before the evaluation. At the end of the day, the FBI neuropsychologist indicated to Nick and me that, upon the request of the prosecutor, he would write a report about his examination to assist the prosecution and the presiding judge.

After waiting with great anxiety every day for the next four months for a response from prosecutors, Nick's lawyers finally initiated a phone call to them. The prosecutors told Nick's lawyers that the FBI neuropsychologist had basically agreed with the defense experts' opinions and test results, as well as their recommendation that Nick not be prosecuted as a criminal but rather be placed on diversion, which would not cause him to be a felon and a registered sex offender for the rest of his life. In spite of what initially appeared to be good news, the prosecutors were not willing to drop their prosecution. Our family was shocked. Not only were the prosecutors disregarding their own expert's assessment, but were also unwilling to request a written report from him. I was starting to wonder why they had even sent Nick to Washington DC in the first place.

Nick's lawyers were sufficiently concerned that they decided to go above the assistant prosecutors who were handling the case and appeal directly to their superior, the US Attorney. A meeting was scheduled with the US Attorney, the chief of the criminal division, and the assistant prosecutors who had been handling Nick's case. At this meeting, Nick's lawyers argued that all the experts, including the government's, had agreed that diversion was an appropriate adjudication for Nick. The US Attorney consented to further consider this matter. Nick's lawyers were encouraged. The prosecutors then called Nick's lawyers later that same day saying that the US Attorney now wanted Nick to be examined by yet another psychologist.

It seemed unfair that Nick was going to have to endure another intense examination, especially so soon after the FBI neuropsychologist's evaluation. At first, the prosecutors told Nick's lawyers that this next examiner should have sufficient expertise in ASDs in order to conduct a fair evaluation. That statement reassured our lawyers that the prosecutors were acting in good faith. However, shortly thereafter, the prosecutors reversed course and told Nick's lawyers they were insisting on a particular forensic psychologist, who was not an expert in ASDs, to conduct the examination. This forensic psychologist was well known and often testified in high profile cases on behalf of the prosecution. After another agonizing four-month wait, the prosecutors finally scheduled an appointment for Nick to see him.

The examination lasted over six hours and included additional psychological testing. A month later, a copy of the forensic psychologist's report was sent directly to Nick's lawyers. The report stated that after the personality tests he performed on Nick:

neither test profile points to the likelihood of antisocial attitudes or behaviors, any tendency to act in defiance of social norms and the rights of others, or any propensity to lose impulse control generally... Mr Dubin's developmental problems, and the limitations they have imposed, may well have a bearing on the behavior in question, namely accessing child pornography.

He concluded his report with important words of advice to the prosecutors:

In fact, there does not appear to be any basis for concluding that [Nick] is at any particular risk of sex offending... What Mr Dubin is accused of doing...is not sexual offending in any case... Mr Dubin faces substantial challenges in making his way in the world, achieving a greater level of social connectedness and independence, and finding ways to cope with the depression and anxiety that his developmental disorder has produced. He had not proceeded without misstep and error, but he does appear to be strongly motivated to do better and to make use of the support and opportunities for advancement he has been given. It is worthwhile, from all points of view, for him to continue without the imposition of new impediments, particularly ones that would limit his access to social support and opportunities for social learning. His path is hard enough as it is.

His recommendation to the prosecutors who had hired him was not to impose any "new impediments" on Nick. The prosecutors rejected that advice, along with the conclusions of the other experts. They again insisted that Nick enter a plea that would require him to be a convicted felon and register as a sex offender. It seems clear that the government's own forensic psychologist did not want this result.

In the end, the prosecutors had Nick submit to two comprehensive examinations by experts they selected and then did not accept the recommendations of these experts. The only option left was for Nick to go to trial. However, after two-and-a-half years of unrelenting stress and anxiety as well as his physical health being negatively impacted, Nick was worn down. He lacked the emotional stability and physical stamina to endure the rigors and uncertainty of a trial. His fate was sealed. He was to become a convicted felon and registered sex offender.

The government's sentencing memorandum

Before a defendant is sentenced in federal court, prosecutors prepare a memorandum providing the judge with pertinent information about the case. In that memorandum, prosecutors in Nick's case acknowledged that his:

> history is replete with difficult and unfortunate hardships directly related to Asperger's Syndrome… That he has… continually suffered from anxiety and depression; symptoms commonly associated with Asperger's Syndrome…and that he has had limited intimate relationships as he suffered with severe social deficits that are at the foundation of the disorder of Autism.

The memorandum also recognized the gap between Nick's intellectual and social development:

> Despite impressive academic and professional accomplishments, Defendant has remained dependent on his parents and his adaptive functions place his general social and emotional development to that of a child… Use of his computer was a way for someone like Nick to learn about sexuality…without suffering the laborious and uncomfortable contact with real people.

In addition, the prosecutors credited Nick for his diligence in seeking the therapeutic help he needed.

> Due to his Asperger's Syndrome, Defendant has regularly participated in therapy and appears to continue to successfully address his particular needs. Defendant has no criminal record and no history of aggression or violence… Defendant has taken steps to help himself beyond what was required of him by Pre-Trial Services. The government is satisfied that Defendant's post-arrest conduct has demonstrated his respect for the law.

The prosecutors' statements about Nick reflect their acceptance of the findings of the experts who examined him: above average intellect; below average adaptive functions; respect for the law; no criminal record; no prior acts of aggression; not a sexual predator; and the progress he made towards rehabilitation. Although prosecutors acknowledged the findings on which the experts based their recommendation not to convict Nick for possession of child pornography, I was deeply saddened that they came to such a different conclusion.

The federal judge before whom Nick appeared at sentencing stated on the record that he was convinced that Nick would not be a repeat offender. He also acknowledged his previous work record history was "impressive."

The impact on our lives

Nick's conviction and registration as a sex offender has shattered our family. Since the day the FBI searched Nick's apartment and throughout the subsequent criminal proceedings, Nick has been severely traumatized and our lives have been turned upside down. Every day since Nick's arrest, I have spent hours with him trying to confront his depression head on, discussing his bleak thoughts, and trying to find hope in a very dark future landscape. It has been a very lonely and scary period that defies most other human experiences.

The federal prosecutors, who have enormous power over people's lives, had the opportunity to see that justice was served in a way that would have both protected the public and prevented imposing an unnecessary and almost insurmountable obstacle on Nick's already challenged life. Their decision has caused great personal suffering and psychological damage to our family.

Advice to parents, mental health professionals, criminal defense lawyers, prosecutors, and judges

I am aware that others throughout this book have offered advice to various groups of people. Without wanting to be redundant, but rather for emphasis, the advice I have to offer is from the perspective of being a lawyer and Nick's father, so I ask that you please keep my unique perspective in mind when reading the following.

To parents

I know the love and dedication that is required of parents raising a child on the autism spectrum. There are so many issues that are extremely difficult to navigate. I have great admiration for parents who work hard to find and pay for necessary services while helping their children deal with the many social, sensory, speech and language, and other issues that can arise. With my deepest respect for these special and dedicated parents, let me offer this advice in light of our family's heart-breaking experience.

- Recognize that your child is a sexual being. Although it may be difficult to deal with your child's sexual issues, don't ignore them, and seek professional help if necessary. Current research indicates that a variety of problems can arise with respect to sexual development for those on the autism spectrum.

- Make clear to your child that certain behaviors could lead to an encounter with the criminal justice system and even to imprisonment. These behaviors include viewing child pornography on the internet, stalking, unwanted touching, having meltdowns in public, and indecent exposure. Your child must understand the severe legal consequences that can occur when these types of charges are brought against people on the autism spectrum who may not understand that they were even committing a criminal act. It may be appropriate to place restraints on your child's computer to ensure only lawful use.

- Nick's case was processed under federal law of the United States. Although most countries criminalize possession of child pornography, the elements of the crime, the possible defenses, and the potential prison sentences are not uniformly followed. Parents should become familiar with the laws pertaining to child pornography in the country in which they reside.

- Be sure your child knows that if ever confronted by the police, with respect to having committed a crime, he or she should be polite and ask for a lawyer to be present without making any further statements. The trusting and naive nature of people on the autism spectrum, who typically want to please authority, make them easy candidates to be taken advantage of by trained police officers who can question them without the protection of a lawyer. The law allows police officers to make certain false statements in order to get a confession that can and will be used against the person. There is also the danger that false confessions can occur. It is always best to have a lawyer present to represent the interests of a person on the autism spectrum before making any statements to law enforcement personnel.

To mental health professionals

Those on the autism spectrum have certain unique needs that even the most experienced therapists may not understand or be familiar with. It is extremely important for therapists who are treating these clients to undertake the responsibility of educating themselves about people with ASD, their sexual and social development, and the proper ways to provide treatment. Dr Klin (August 4, 2008) states:

> Individuals with Asperger Syndrome benefit from behavioral intervention that provides them with clear instruction, explicit rules, and an understanding of the reasons for those rules... This intervention can be done by an experienced mental health professional, and there are specific curricula for such interventions in the area of sexuality... The individual's conduct should be monitored for compliance and positive feedback should be provided in response to his understanding of the situation.

It is essential for therapists to check in regularly with their ASD clients about sexual issues and to repeatedly reinforce the reasons for not viewing child pornography, including the harm done to the children during the production of this material. Dr Klin (August 4, 2008) explains:

> Because of their disability, individuals with Asperger Syndrome would be likely to miss the connection between consuming

child pornography and supporting the exploitation of children. Because of their difficulty reading emotion and understanding non-verbal communication, the person with AS would have difficulty recognizing or would entirely miss the emotions of fear, anxiety and discomfort on the faces of children in the pictures... Non-verbal communication that most people recognize and respond to intuitively is unseen by those with autism spectrum disorders.

This is the concept of "mindblindness," which Dr Attwood referred to in his chapter as "impaired Theory of Mind" and explains how there can be a disconnect between intelligence and social understanding.

To deter the ASD client from viewing child pornography, the therapist must clearly explain that the FBI monitors the activities of those who download child pornography, which could lead to an FBI raid and an arrest. The therapist must also spell out the specific legal consequences that can occur after an arrest, including wearing a tether, having an officer make regular unannounced home visits, facing the real possibility of going to prison, and being a convicted felon requiring registration as a sex offender. In addition, the therapist must not allow the numerous life problems that confront an ASD patient to distract from dealing with sexual issues.

Academic psychologists also need to establish and support a joint program in higher education that combines expertise and knowledge in ASDs with human sexuality. It is difficult to find an expert in one of these fields who also has expertise in the other field. Yet for the proper therapeutic treatment of people on the autism spectrum, the treating professional needs to be knowledgeable in both disciplines.

To criminal defense lawyers

It is imperative that those in the criminal justice system be aware of the current statistic from the Centers for Disease Control and Prevention that one out of every forty-two boys is now being diagnosed on the autism spectrum (Centers for Disease Control and Prevention, 2014; Falco, 2014). Based on the information presented in this chapter, a high likelihood exists that there will be a much greater interface between the criminal justice system and those on the autism spectrum. There are a whole host of issues that criminal defense lawyers will need to understand in defending autistic clients. Nick was fortunate to have criminal defense lawyers who undertook a comprehensive study of autism and how that condition and resulting life history was related to the criminal charges in question. The absence of an attorney willing to understand the relationship of autism to the criminal charges would have significantly increased the likelihood that Nick would have been sent to prison. I am eternally grateful that he was not incarcerated. Knowing my son as I do and his disability, I feel strongly Nick would not have been able to survive that experience. There are many legal questions that are currently being raised throughout the country about how autism can impact criminal responsibility. It is critical to understand this cutting-edge issue and not to handle a case in a one-size-fits-all fashion.

Defense lawyers also need to be aware that those on the autism spectrum who are charged with a crime will be highly anxious, depressed, and in need of compassionate counsel. Lawyers need to take into account the emotional needs of the autistic client who finds dealing with uncertainty, especially of this magnitude, unbearable.

To prosecutors

Having been a lawyer for almost five decades, I have seen how being a long-time prosecutor can cause one to see all people charged with crimes as dangerous criminals who need to be convicted and shown no mercy. This attitude can deprive a prosecutor of appropriate compassion when it comes to exercising prosecutorial discretion. Law without compassion can be cruel. Compassion without law can be dangerous. I urge prosecutors to keep in check the tremendous power they possess and use discretion wisely when dealing with people on the autism spectrum charged with crimes. Compassion can often help in making good decisions and achieving justice with the finest degree of discernment. When appropriate, prosecutors can help people on the autism spectrum rehabilitate their lives, rather than labeling them as criminals. Justice doesn't always mean getting a felony conviction. As Dr Klin (August 4, 2008) stated:

> While the criminal justice system judges conduct assuming that adults possess reasonable common sense and an understanding of what is right and what is wrong, the ability of the individual

with Asperger Syndrome to make those judgments is severely disrupted. It is not that persons with Asperger Syndrome lack values. Rather, their developmental disorder impacts their appreciation of these things without explicit instruction or clear rules.

I strongly recommend that prosecutors read the following excerpts from a letter that Dr Klin wrote to his colleagues at the Yale Child Studies Center (August 22, 2008) to address a "public policy crisis" faced by individuals with AS and their families. The letter offers a clear perspective and sound advice to attorneys prosecuting AS defendants in child pornography cases.

> The prosecution of child pornography cases is a high priority for both the Department of Justice and state prosecutors. The state and federal laws originally targeted those who produced and distributed child pornography, which in turn is based on the raw sexual exploitation of children. The laws are also directed at those who purchase child pornography, on the reasoning that purchasers provide the economic incentive to produce child pornography. However, in recent years many prosecutions are directed at those who have obtained such material for free over the Internet, or simply viewed them on the Internet.
>
> The basis for spreading of the net so far is the belief that those who have an interest in such materials are pedophiles and present a risk to children. Indeed, this presumption of dangerousness is so strong that there is no process in child pornography prosecutions for distinguishing between those who are truly predatory pedophiles and those who are not pedophiles, with no interest in inappropriate contact with children. It is no defense to a charge of possessing child pornography that the accused is not a danger to children...
>
> As a result of all this, the experience in most cases we are aware of is that it is very difficult to get prosecutors to forego prosecution in these cases. Prosecutors are focused on the possibility, even remote, that an accused might be a danger to children. There is tremendous political pressure to be harsh on "child pornographers" and there is virtually no voice for restraint.

Like most people, prosecutors judge behavior from a perspective which assumes common sense and an understanding of what is acceptable and what is not. When it comes to defendants with disabilities, and there are many, prosecutors often view this as something which may evoke sympathy for the plight of the accused, but which does not affect culpability. Prosecutors find the features of Asperger's Syndrome especially hard to accept in child pornography cases because they run counter to the presumption of dangerousness. They find it hard to grasp that the suspect who appears high functioning is so socially immature and unable to pick up on the social taboos and legal rules which these laws enforce.

Having literally demonized those possessing child pornography as child predators, it is hard to accept the idea that the accused Asperger's patient is, in such significant ways (such as in their severe limitations in understanding implicit mores and regulations that are common sense in our culture— and from the stand point of social judgment) just a child himself whose interest in sexual images of children does not fit the stereotype. They find it hard to accept what is typically true, that all such an individual needed was to have been told very concretely, very literally, and very firmly, that this behavior is unacceptable...

The outcomes of the case involving Asperger's sufferers are deeply tragic... These individuals would be required to register as a sex offender after completion of their sentences. In most states they would be unable to reside near any school, playground, or day care center, which gets very problematic if they need to live with family, as many Asperger's patients do, and their residence falls within a prohibited area.

All these consequences would be difficult enough for a neurotypical person. For the individual with Asperger's Syndrome, these impediments will be piled on top of disabilities that, on their own, will be already difficult to manage throughout their lives.

Federal and state prosecutors have the authority to "defer prosecution." That is, before or after arrest they can reach an agreement with a person that he will comply with certain conditions, over a period of usually up to 18 months, whereupon the charges would be dismissed. This would allow a prosecutor time to ensure that the individual is getting treatment, and does not present a risk to children, before writing off the charges. We need the Department of Justice and state prosecutors to adopt a policy of deferring prosecution in appropriate cases.

To judges

Judges also need to use their discretion wisely. They have a tremendous amount of power over the lives of people who come before them. There are people on the autism spectrum who pose no danger whatsoever and are still incarcerated for long periods of time and are required to register as sex offenders upon release. Sending harmless people on the spectrum to prison illustrates that prosecutors and judges lack an understanding of the lifelong and devastating impact this punishment will have on them and their families.

When the federal judge sentenced Nick, he said he had learned something new from reading the pre-sentence report, which was that Asperger's was neurological in origin and not a mental illness. This judge showed that he had a willingness to learn about ASD. I wish all judges would adopt this same attitude.

A plea for change in the legal system

Mark Mahoney, an attorney in Buffalo, NY, who has defended several AS defendants in child pornography cases, wrote an extensive document entitled *Asperger's Syndrome and the Criminal Law: The Special Case of Child Pornography* (2009) which is available on the internet. Here is the conclusion to his well-researched document:

> There is no tragedy without hope. Individuals with AS and their families hope for a "normal" life, but they have great difficulties in achieving that dream. In part this is due not to the inherent nature of the disability, but the misunderstanding of the individual by those who cannot understand how a person with apparently normal intelligence could not appreciate the oddness, or the apparently deviant appearance of their

behavior. There cannot be a more tragic example of this than the AS individual who, because of his greater skill and comfort and trust in the world of his computer and the internet, and because of his obliviousness to legally-created taboos, wanders into child pornography. He is a victim of a marketing scheme to which his disability makes him the most susceptible and he is at the same time most easily caught because of his naiveté as to how his computer has been opened to the world. At that point he is exposed to criminal conviction and the harshest civil disabilities devised which can literally ruin his entire life.

While prosecutors and judges "have heard it all before" when it comes to people "excusing" misbehavior, including the possession of child pornography, the unique features predominant in AS, together with the backdrop of hysteria, sentiment, and fervor concerning child pornography, create a "perfect storm" in which AS individuals and their families are engulfed. This unique diagnosis calls upon prosecutors and courts to draw distinctions between dangerous and non-dangerous offenders and between those who may access offending depictions because they need to as opposed to those who simply do not know better. Generally AS individuals should not be charged at all. It is totally unnecessary. If they are charged every effort should be expended to avoid civil disabilities of incarceration, and to insure treatment suitable to the AS diagnosis.

In order to avoid such "perfect storms" the "experts" and advocates in the field, trying to bring hope to these individuals, need to help inform the legislators, prosecutors, and judges, so that they can make informed decisions in this area so ripe for tragedy.

The road ahead

Standing beside Nick at his sentencing hearing in federal court was an excruciatingly painful moment for me. My heart stopped beating when the court clerk called out, "United States v. Nicolas Dubin." I thought to myself: *I will not accept, and in fact, I explicitly reject the United States government publically labeling Nick as a felon and a sex offender.*

As with every other instance in his life where someone has misunderstood him, I am encouraging Nick not to let others define him as a person. I hope all parents of children on the autism spectrum will reinforce this important message to their children: do not let other people define you. Nick has been given a label that doesn't fit him. My goals for now, and in the long road ahead, are to help Nick believe in himself again, to increase awareness of this important subject, and to advocate for change in the legal system.

References

Carley, M.J., Gerhardt, P., Jekel, D., Klin, A., Moreno, S., Rosenwald, L., Schissel, P., Sherry, L. and Volkmar, F. (2008) *Principles for Prosecutors Considering Child Pornography Charges Against Persons with Asperger's Syndrome.* Available at www.harringtonmahoney.com/documents/Principles%20for%20Prosecutors%20-%209-14-08.pdf, accessed on March 8, 2014.

Centers for Disease Control and Prevention (2014) "CDC estimates 1 in 68 children has been identified with autism spectrum disorder." *Centers for Disease Control and Prevention,* March 27. Available at www.cdc.gov/media/releases/2014/p0327-autism-spectrum-disorder.html, accessed on May 13, 2014.

Debbaudt, D., Mesibov, G. and Taylor, K. (2009) *Asperger Syndrome in the Criminal Justice System.* Watertown, MA: modified and reformatted for an AS population by Nomi Kain. Available at www.aane.org/asperger_resources/articles/miscellaneous/as_in_the_criminal_justice_system.html, accessed on May 13, 2014.

Falcor, M. (2014) "Autism ratse now 1 in 68 US children: CDC." *CNN,* March 28. Available at http://edition.cnn.com/2014/03/27/health/cdc-autism, accessed on May 13, 2014.

Fenclau, E., Huang, A., Hughes, T., Lehman, C., Marshall, S., Paserba, D., Sutton, L., Talkington, V., Taormina, R. and Walters, J. (2012) "Identifying individuals with autism in a state facility for adolescents adjudicated as sexual offenders: a pilot study." *Focus on Autism and Other Developmental Disabilities 28,* 3, 1–9.

Gougeon, N. (2010) "Sexuality and autism: a critical review of small selected literature using a social-relational model of disability." *American Journal of Sexuality Education 5,* 4, 328–361.

Klin, A. (2008) Letter to United States District Judge, the Hon. Richard Bennett *et al. Sentencing Recommendation of a Defendant on the Autism Spectrum for Possession of Internet Child Pornography.* August 4.

Klin, A. (2008) Letter from Dr Klin to Autism Organizations and Colleagues, August 22.

Mahoney, M. (2009) *Asperger's Syndrome and Criminal Law: The Special Case of Child Pornography.* Available at www.harringtonmahoney.com/documents/Asperger%20Syndrome%20and%20the%20Criminal%20Law%20v26.pdf.

Parker, M. (2008) "Autism Principles for Prosecutors." In University of North Carolina School of Government (2008) *Joint Study Committee on Autism Spectrum Disorders and Public Safety.* Chapel Hill, NC: University of North Carolina School of Government.

Robison, J. E. (2013) "Autism and porn: a problem no one talks about." *Psychology Today,* August 6.

Solomon, A. (2012) *Far From the Tree: Parents, Children and the Search For Identity.* New York, NY: Scribner, A Division of Simon and Schuster, Inc.

SEX EDUCATION AND INTERVENTION

Isabelle Hénault

CHAPTER 1

Introduction

In the last few years, many individuals with Asperger's syndrome (AS) have faced legal problems that were linked to sexual behavior, making Nick Dubin's story far from unique. Other adults with AS have also found themselves in inappropriate or illegal situations. When it comes to sexual issues, discomfort, negative judgment, and lack of support can increase the social isolation and stigmatization of these individuals.

When I heard about Nick Dubin's situation, I welcomed the opportunity to contribute to his book. As a psychologist, I often meet adolescents and adults with AS who are experiencing difficulties with interpersonal relationships, mixed with curiosity about sexuality. Most of them experience social isolation and rejection from their peer group on a daily basis, and have never had access to sex education.

A person with AS is intrinsically naive in terms of sexual knowledge and experience. This naivety increases his or her vulnerability, his or her risk of becoming a victim, and the chance that he or she may display inappropriate sexual behaviors. Learning about sexuality is one of the best ways to prevent such negative outcomes. Overprotection by families and professionals sometimes increases the gap between what the individual should know about sexuality and his or her actual knowledge. Thus, prevention is the appropriate solution. It enables the individual to learn in a positive environment as well as gain experience and independence. An adapted sex education lesson plan should be part of the curriculum for every individual on the autism spectrum. Many concepts need to be explored and understood: limits and boundaries, appropriate and inappropriate behaviors, Theory of Mind and the notion of consent, illegal behaviors and their consequences, body parts, hygiene, self-esteem, intimacy, steps in a relationship, expression of emotion, communication, and positive relationships.

This part of the book will first describe the factors contributing to inappropriate and sometimes illegal sexual situations. Following chapters will explore prevention and education about healthy sexuality. Many strategies and programs developed and adapted for individuals with AS have been helpful in terms of sex education and the prevention of illegal and inappropriate sexual conduct. By improving their knowledge of sexual development, many adolescents and adults with AS will gain confidence in social interactions and, ultimately, better manage their social integration.

The appendix at the end of this chapter provides an example of sex education guidelines to be used by professionals in group homes, institutions, and other environments that offer support and services to individuals with AS.

CHAPTER 2

Factors Influencing Sexual Development

Over the last few years, several authors have become increasingly aware that the sexual development of individuals diagnosed with autism spectrum disorder (ASD) and AS is a subject that deserves particular attention. This led to proposals of various intervention strategies, therapeutic tools, and sociosexual educational programs adapted to these individuals. Several distinct factors must be considered in order to understand the complexity of the sexual development of individuals with AS (Griffiths, Quinsey and Hingsburger, 1989). A satisfied and adapted sexuality and sexual lifestyle is an important component of healthy development and a good indicator of quality of life (Hollomotz, 2011). Recent research on the differential effects of autism and Down's syndrome upon sexual behavior reports that adolescents with AS have less sexual education than typical adolescents, more inappropriate sexual behavior, and fewer positive social interactions (Ginevra, Nota and Stokes, unpublished). These behavioral factors obviously increase the social isolation and vulnerability of these young people.

Young individuals with AS are often viewed as asexual, as if their condition prevents them from having a sexual life. Unfortunately, this sometimes leads to a denial of their sexual development by their families and friends, and limits their supportive social network. This raises an important issue: with whom can they discuss their sexual experiences (or absence of) and their sexual feelings? If peers and parents feel awkward about the topic of sexuality, the teenager may rapidly withdraw from subsequent social contacts involving sexuality. Emotions associated with sexuality are equally ambivalent; they are given many warnings to protect them from abusive situations or behaviors. These warnings may create a high level of irrational fear or anxiety, which affects the teenager's desire and willingness to understand his or her own sexuality.

Gender segregation

Separating male and female residents in group homes or in activities can also be problematic because homosexual and masturbatory behaviors may emerge as a result of unsatisfactory (or lack of) contact with people of the opposite sex. If sexual segregation disappears in favor of inclusion, then the sexual behaviors of people with autism will be more likely to resemble those of the general population.

Impoverished environments

The lack of opportunity to discuss sensitive topics openly and freely frequently occurs in residential establishments and is sometimes reinforced by staff members, especially with regard to sexuality. Formal or informal rules can be introduced. If there are no predetermined rules, who determines if a behavior is acceptable or not? Does a person with autism receive a variety of different and inconsistent messages? There appear to be no norms regarding sexual conduct in institutions or group homes. Punishment of behavior is frequent, which diminishes the opportunity to develop more responsible behavior. Teams working with individuals who have AS should create an atmosphere that promotes responsibility by preventing sexual abuse, promoting sexual education, and recognizing the possibility of sexual contact between them (Griffiths *et al.*, 2002). An example of the kind of sexual guidelines that can be employed in these environments is presented in the Appendix (Taillefer *et al.*, 2013).

Intimacy

This can be defined as the possibility of being alone with a partner, be it for emotional or sexual reasons. Intimacy is the foundation upon which relationships are built. It can be experienced at several levels:

relational, emotional, and physical. Intimate moments may not only be opportunities for sexual contact for people with AS, but they may also serve to expand interpersonal experiences. One goal would be to provide the young people with time and opportunities to develop intimate relationships with others. Adolescents should have the chance to explore the different aspects of intimacy while being guided by a responsible adult. Here too, the tendency to overprotect quickly arises. Limiting experiences will in no way be helpful as it only places the youth in a more vulnerable state.

People often exhibit stereotyped attitudes concerning the rights of people with AS. It is important to firmly state that these individuals have the same right to a normal sexual life as do individuals in the general population. This means that each individual's needs and sexual desires must be considered. Education and intervention programs dealing with sexuality can only come into play once this right is fully respected.

There are other complicating factors linked to the sexual development of individuals with AS that can become a source of conflict.

Gender identity

Adolescence is commonly viewed as a developmental stage where gender identity in general is questioned. Belonging to the male or female sex determines many of our behaviors and our place in the social world. As such, neurotypical adolescents will usually have the desire to belong to the subgroup with which they identify. This sets into motion a whole series of protocols and changes related to dress code, musical preferences, interests, and behavioral repertoire. Some adolescents with AS may experience gender identity in a different way. Many clinical experiences have led to the hypothesis that young people with AS exhibit more flexibility in the experience of gender (masculine and feminine characteristics or being gender-neutral). They are less attuned to social rules and do not feel the same pressures to belong to or affiliate with any particular group. Their tendency to isolate themselves can become a source of conflict if the individual has no bearings with respect to a sense of belonging. Sexual preference does not seem to obey the strict social rules typically associated with adolescence. The general categories are more flexible and more movement between categories has been observed in individuals with AS (Hénault, 2006). It therefore appears that some individuals with AS respect their own sense of identity over socially determined norms.

Social imitation

Rituals and routines make up the behavioral repertoire that provides adolescents with a sense of security. The impaired social development of people with AS can lead to difficulties in starting and maintaining interpersonal relationships. Adolescents tend to imitate their peers' behavior without necessarily decoding its inherent complexity. As such, they can reproduce an observed behavior without considering or fully understanding the context in which it took place. For example, a person with AS who has seen a couple kissing in the street could attempt to kiss the first girl he meets. An adolescent could also repeat a form of touch that he experienced. Failing to consider the context in which these behaviors take place can increase the likelihood that an inappropriate sexual behavior will occur.

Understanding of complex interpersonal relationships

Individuals with AS have difficulty decoding the messages that are transmitted during interactions with several individuals or in conversational groups. Words and sentences with double meanings lead to confusion. In addition, non-verbal communication (which acts as a parallel language) is also difficult for them to detect and interpret. As such, a simple conversation can easily turn into a nightmarish experience. Even more disturbing, sexuality is filled with subtleties in small gestures and intentions that must be decoded on a second level. Adolescents with AS report that their interactions felt as if they were in the presence of someone who was talking an unknown dialect: "It is like learning a new language each time." Some individuals learn to detect and decode specific cues (key words, precise gestures, intonations of voice). Nonetheless, when they are too rigid, conflicts are likely to occur.

Sexuality on the internet

Unable to share experiences and knowledge with other teenagers, many teens and young adults with AS choose to learn by themselves on the internet. Accessing pornography for free on the internet has become a typical experience for many individuals, including those with AS. Although their first encounter is usually motivated by a genuine and positive need to learn, internet research about sexuality will expose them to pornographic websites that display explicitly sexual (if not extreme) pictures and videos. Because most individuals with AS have a tendency to take information in a literal way, they are particularly vulnerable. If there is a lack of parental surveillance and support, the teenager will access these sites without any background information to serve as a point of reference. Due to the lack of experience, sexuality can quickly become associated with pornography. In addition, this explicit visual material can be appealing and exciting at first, and one site can lead to another with more and more pornographic material. Even if the individual did not access "extreme" websites, this quick, easy, and intense exposure to pornographic material can become a habit or a routine, especially when sexual pleasure is associated with it.

The internet contains millions of sites with sexual content; some is considered pornography, but purely educational information about sex is also available. Given that individuals with AS may lack judgment and experience when it comes to understanding the material they encounter, supervision by parents and educators is essential in preventing the inadvertent discovery of illegal pornography. In addition, viewing sexual images on the internet during masturbation often becomes habitual and can form part of a ritual that is then difficult to break. Repeated exposure to sexual content also increases the risk of developing specific sexual interests, along with sexual obsessions and compulsions.

The presence of sexual predators who tend to frequent sites where chatting or other encounters take place is an additional risk (Carnes, Delmonico and Griffin, 2007; Edmonds and Worton, 2006). Individuals with AS are more vulnerable to such risks, therefore rules must be explained clearly to ensure their security, and supervision must be constant. In their book, Edmonds and Worton (2006) list a series of suggestions to ensure the protection of those with autism and AS. They suggest, for example, parental or peer supervision to increase safety and ensure that limits are placed on chatting. According to guidelines taught in a number of sexual education programs, conversations held over the internet that include sexual content (either words, intentions, images, or videos) must not be tolerated. This also includes meeting an individual (even one who is considered to be a friend) if this person was met through the internet, unless accompanied by parents or a responsible adult and in a public place. Under no circumstances should personal information be shared (name, address, telephone number, and bank or credit card information).

Because individuals with AS have difficulty understanding or perceiving negative intentions in other people, they often misread intentions and follow instructions in a literal way. In this respect, the internet can be a real problem. Although no intimate or sexual pictures should be published on the internet (e.g. Facebook), individuals with AS may be convinced to provide intimate details or sexual pictures upon request from a stranger, without thinking about consequences. In the somewhat more neutral environment of online chat rooms, they also need to be aware of specific rules, such as never provide private or personal data (bank account numbers, telephone, passwords, etc.). Teaching the consequences and dangers related to sharing personal information on the internet, and giving formal instructions about safe behavior, is essential to protecting individuals with AS from trouble and abuse.

Individuals with AS need to know what information is appropriate for sharing through social media and other internet sites and what is inappropriate.

Some appropriate messages and news include:

- general pictures from holidays or news from a trip or vacation

- invitations to special events or activities

- general news about school or work.

Definitely inappropriate messages and information include:

- personal details such as address or contact details

- intimate pictures and information (about relationship, partner, etc.)

- any sexual content that includes messages, pictures, or videos that are sent or requested

- threats of any kind about school, work, an organization, or an individual

- asking someone for intimate or sexual details

- downloading pictures or videos of child or juvenile pornography

- sending or sharing files, pictures or videos of child or juvenile pornography.

Relationships

The topic of relationships raises a lot of questions regarding the adjustments that may be needed between a neurotypical and an AS partner, or between two AS individuals. Within a relationship, the expression of behavioral traits associated with AS varies depending on many factors such as previous experience, disclosure and acceptance of the diagnosis, quality of communication skills, family situation, mutual support, motivation of partners, etc.

For some AS people, intimacy remains a rather vague concept grounded on very few concrete things. They do not refuse to share intimacy with a partner, but some of them have little experience regarding interpersonal relationships. The lack of privacy and the poor quality of relationships between partners are major sources of discontent among couples who seek counseling. Some neurotypical partners report that the AS partner (male or female) often assumes that the well being of the couple comes down to an active sex life. However, satisfactory sexual intercourse (in terms of frequency and quality) is not a guarantee of success in the intimate life of a couple. Sexuality is only one of the components of intimacy. This "concrete and tangible" understanding of intimacy is quite characteristic of the AS profile.

Several books have been written that address the concerns of Asperger's couples. *The Partner's Guide to Asperger's Syndrome* (Moreno, Wheeler and Parkinson, 2012); *Aspergers in Love* (Aston, 2003), and *Loving Someone with Asperger's Syndrome* (Ariel, 2012) are useful references both for professionals and for couples. Domestic dynamics must be addressed by taking into account the AS profile. Rigidity, special interests, and rituals may sometimes lead to unusual requests from the AS partner. In one way or another, the other partner will have to adjust to this reality. These characteristics are inherent in the AS condition, and they can hardly be ignored without compromising the relationship. Emotional communication, sexual behavior, desire, and empathy are all themes that deserve to be addressed concretely and precisely during therapy. However, the main and most important ingredient remains the full commitment of partners. The request for therapy illustrates the couple's desire for change and sharing. Both partners must be motivated, because they need to invest time and energy if they want their relationship to change. Therapy must extend beyond the walls of the session in the office; discussions and exercises should be completed during the week. Change may sometimes be painful, especially for the AS partner. Accustomed to certain routines, he or she will have to consider and accept requests and desires from his or her partner. Sex therapy incorporates all the components of sexuality and has to be adapted to the reality of the couple. The task is sometimes laborious but the investment is worth it.

Masturbation

For many adolescents and their families, the topic of masturbation is taboo. However, neglecting to address this important subject could lead to inappropriate behavior (e.g. masturbating in public) or misuse of material (e.g. illegal pictures or websites). Masturbation is the most common sexual behavior reported by adolescents with AS. Discovery of one's body and accompanying pleasant sensations is quite widespread. In itself, self-stimulation is not a problem especially if expressed within a given framework. However, behavioral problems related to masturbation are often observed in individuals with AS. Hellemans and Deboutte (2002) have found that public masturbation is the most frequent inappropriate behavior expressed in the ASD population.

Masturbation can become a sexual compulsion or a source of distraction (just like any other activity). Some individuals achieve such pleasure that they constantly seek to reproduce it in order to distract themselves. They tend to engage in this behavior when their level of general stimulation is not high enough (at school, work, or during free time). In general, teens masturbate one to five times per day. Several factors contribute to the frequency of self-stimulation. The high levels of sex hormones (testosterone and estrogen) characteristic of adolescence cause an increase in sexual desire. Orgasm and the physical pleasure that accompanies masturbation serve as powerful reinforcement. Masturbation is usually discovered quite naturally, but individuals may sometimes need information, support, and intervention. Shyness, shame, or guilt can sometimes interfere. Messages about masturbation can be contradictory: on the one hand it can be considered dirty and unhealthy and on the other, a natural and desirable way of discovering one's body. According to Hingsburger (1995), some behaviors or attitudes can lead to problematic masturbation:

- the individual masturbates incessantly

- masturbation that does not end with ejaculation

- the individual masturbates but believes that it is bad, dirty, immoral, dangerous, disgusting, etc.

- injury occurs from masturbation (due to overly intense stimulation)

- public masturbation

- the individual is afraid of masturbation.

Adolescents or adults with AS may display these above-mentioned behaviors or have difficulty forming their own opinion about the subject. Blum and Blum (1981; as cited in Hingsburger, 1995) suggest five learning objectives with respect to masturbation:

1. learning that masturbation is a normal and healthy behavior

2. learning the appropriate time and place in which to engage in the behavior (private versus public places)

3. debunking myths and their effects

4. introducing the notion that sexual fantasies can accompany masturbation

5. learning what kind of stimulation leads to pleasure.

This kind of education allows individuals with AS to express their emotions and any difficulties that they may have with self-stimulation. In some cases, stimulation is inadequate or objects that can harm the genitals are used. Providing clear and concrete information about safety is essential.

Here is an example of how to use a protocol for masturbation.

1. Discuss medication and side effects if necessary.

2. If you are a professional, write a contract with your organization so it is aware of your education strategies and interventions.

3. Discuss and teach private body parts with pictures or drawings.

4. Teach the difference between private and public places.

5. Establish a sequence and times in a schedule (to avoid inappropriate behaviors).

6. Teach the steps and the sequence of the procedure and the positive aspects of using these steps (private, alone in a bedroom, etc.).

7. K-Y Jelly (water lubricant) can be used to accentuate the feelings and pleasure, if required.

8. If the individual needs more visual support, use a plastic model of genitals to teach all the steps of the masturbation sequence.

9. The DVDs *Finger Tips* (Hingsburger and Harr, 2000) and *Hand Made Love* (Hingsburger, 1995) from www.diverse-city.com can be used to review the steps.

10. Practice all these steps many times (as a sequence) until the individual fully integrates them as a sequence.

CHAPTER 3

Inappropriate Sexual Behaviors

Various forms of inappropriate sexual behaviors can be part of the sexual repertoire of individuals with ASD and AS. The majority of these behaviors consist of sexual acts performed in public, touching or fondling, lack of respect for consent, sexual assault, excessive or inadequate masturbation, sexual obsessions, and compulsions (Haracopos and Pedersen, 1999; Ruble and Dalrymple, 1993). The lack of sociosexual knowledge is always the major issue, as a lack of understanding or a misinterpretation of social and sexual contexts often explains why inappropriate acts are performed. In addition, many AS individuals get confused when it comes to issues of privacy and intimacy, and behaviors of an intimate nature. An exhaustive, detailed, and concrete description of sexual acts and intimate areas of the body is the best way to prevent inappropriate behaviors.

AS also affects the notion of consent. This is related to diminished Theory of Mind skills (i.e. one's ability to recognize different mental states and to attribute thoughts, beliefs, and emotions to others). Specifically, the individual with AS may sometimes assume that others share his or her thoughts and desires without first inquiring as to whether this is the case. Limited Theory of Mind skills thus lead to poor judgment, which explains many inappropriate sexual acts.

Restricted interest and sexual obsessions

Another source of inappropriate sexual behavior is the fact that individuals with AS have a propensity for repetitive and ritualistic activities. While this part of their behavioral repertoire makes them feel safe, it may become problematic when sexuality becomes their special circumscribed interest. If it is a source of pleasure and satisfaction, it is then difficult to curb, modify, or restrain this interest.

However, as long as the sexual interest doesn't cause any harm to the individual or to others, it is important to limit but not forbid it. Just as for other interests, to forbid it will only serve to make it more interesting. It is important to remember that a surge in sexual interest during adolescence is quite common in most neurotypical individuals. The mix of curiosity and excitement makes sexuality all the more attractive. This developmental stage is perfectly normal and even desirable. The need to explore has to be respected (within reasonable limits) because it also illustrates an interest towards others. It leads to socialization and to the development of friendships or intimate relationships. Individuals with AS may or may not have this need for closeness, but if they do, they should be allowed to experience it.

Although this phenomenon is not present in all individuals with AS, sexuality can sometimes take on an added dimension and become a true obsession. Little empirical data exists, but the author's clinical observations have made it possible to detect this phenomenon in some individuals. Obsessions are characterized as uncontrollable, disproportionate desires that are often aczcompanied by anxiety. As the person's circumscribed interest, sexuality becomes the only source of stimulation to the detriment of all other activities. The obsession is expressed through a variety of behaviors: use of pornographic materials (magazines, the internet, etc.), voyeurism, compulsive masturbation, seeking sexual contact, desire for closeness, and repetitive fantasies, etc. If these obsessions are not satisfied (which is likely), it can generate frustration, isolation, and a depressed state.

When the obsession is accompanied by anxiety, the individual's universe revolves around sexuality and has a detrimental effect on everything else: work, their partner, and other activities. Take the following example in which an individual with AS watches four hours of internet pornography per day, masturbates at work during his breaks, constantly seeks sexual contact with women, and talks about the different sexual fantasies/scenarios that he would like to experience. Given that it is obviously impossible to live one's sexuality at such a pace, anxiety will be a logical result. A variety of observations can be made to determine if an individual has lost control. The following were elaborated by Carnes (1989):

- The individual has difficulty resisting potential harmful sexual impulses, urges, or temptations (obsession).

- The individual feels an increase in tension and/or anxiety prior to acting out. The purpose of the act is to decrease this tension (compulsion).

- The individual experiences pleasure and tension release when the compulsive behavior is performed, but can feel guilt and/or regret immediately afterwards.

- Repeated efforts to reduce, control, or stop the behavior have been unsuccessful.

- Sexual activities occupy most of the individual's time and interfere with work and other obligations.

- The sexual behaviors occur regardless of physical problems (irritation, genital pain due to repetitive gestures), financial problems (high cost of pornographic material) or problems with their relationship partner.

- The individual becomes irritable and distressed if the sexual behaviors cannot be performed.

These signs and symptoms must persist for at least one month and appear repeatedly over a long period of time. In order to fully understand their own sexual functioning, individuals with AS need to have sexual experiences. Given the uniqueness of each individual, sexuality can take on a variety of forms. Overprotection only serves to increase undesirable behaviors since the forbidden typically fuels desire. The questions and suggestions listed below should be considered if sexuality has taken on the form of an obsession.

- What sexual behaviors are involved?

- How long has the obsession been present?

- Under what circumstances does the obsession express itself (time of day, preceding and following which activities, involvement of individuals)?

- What purpose does the obsession serve?

- How does the individual behave when he/she talks about the obsession?

- What emotions accompany the repetitive behavior(s) (anxiety, anger, sadness, fear, joy, excitement, etc.)?

With the above information, a *functional analysis* of the obsession can be conducted. Here are some possible interpretations.

- Sexuality is the only source of satisfaction, pleasure, excitement, or gratification.

- The sexual behavior decreases the adolescent's anxiety (especially in situations where a lot is expected of him or her.

- Sexuality becomes a way to challenge authority or what is forbidden.

- Sexuality activity is a way of behaving like an adult (the adolescent doesn't want to be considered a child).

- Sexual contacts stimulate the sensory systems (tactile, visual, olfactory). An intervention strategy based on stimulation may be necessary if the individual with AS is hyposensitive. This would allow him or her to tolerate a minimum of stimulation.

- Sexuality becomes a symptom of another underlying conflict (search for identity, frustration, peer rejection, romantic failures, or social isolation).

- Individuals with AS may view a sexual behavior as having the same value as any other behavior. The differences are associated with sexual behaviors (social context, emotions involved, respecting social norms).

- A sexual obsession, like the majority of obsessions, can provide security.

CHAPTER 4

Intervention and Programs

Sexual education has both short- and long-term goals. In the short term, it allows adaptive sexual behaviors to emerge with respect to communication, emotions, and interpersonal relationships. Over the longer term, adolescents and adults with ASD will be in a better position to understand what interpersonal relationships consist of and will engage in appropriate behaviors in a variety of relationship contexts. They should also be able to explain what is meant by a sexual relationship, how it unfolds, and the circumstances (time, place, appropriate individuals) under which it is possible for a sexual relationship to take place, all while conducting themselves in a manner that is consistent with the situation. Finally, these individuals will understand what is meant by informed consent in the context of a sexual relationship (Tremblay, Desjardins and Gagnon, 1993). The ultimate goal is to allow individuals with ASD to fully experience social integration and healthy sexuality, and access a better quality of life.

The first step in intervention and sexual education programs involves teaching general knowledge, which is tailored to the individual's chronological and developmental age. This information allows the individual to make informed choices. It also enables the person to better understand the limits, within his or her learned behaviors, that can be explored and experienced, while respecting his or her own values and those of others. The goal of the intervention is both to provide a structure for appropriate sexual behaviors and to offer many opportunities for learning and obtaining enriching experiences.

The following themes, which are adapted to the reality of adolescents and adults with AS, cover many of the characteristics linked to their social and sexual development:

- information on nocturnal emissions

- the value of, and stages involved in, making decisions

- intimacy: both private and non-private parts of the body; different environments

- sexual health and initial examination of genital organs— or gynecological exam

- communication: interpersonal, intimate, love, and friendly relationships

- the effect of alcohol and drugs on the ability to make decisions

- sexual relations and other sexual behaviors

- self-stimulation (masturbation)

- sexual orientation and identity

- planning for pregnancy, menstruation, and parental responsibilities

- condoms, contraception, and the prevention of sexually transmitted diseases (STDs)

- hygiene

- friendship: recognition of abusive/unfriendly relationships

- dangerous relationships: age difference, intention, bullying, aggression

- qualities of a healthy relationship: sharing, communication, pleasure, interest, respect

- intensity of relationships: finding a balance and learning the limits

- social skills: presentation, interactions, reciprocity, sharing, etc.

- boundaries and the notion of informed consent

- sexuality on the internet (rules, boundaries, laws, regulations, consequences).

The objectives of the intervention and education program aim primarily to help the individual:

- gain knowledge about social and sexual expectations in the adolescent years

- cope with changes

- develop one's own limits and judgment

- decode situations (interpersonal and intimate contexts)

- improve social and sexual skills

- decrease problem behaviors and inappropriate sexual conducts

- empower the adolescent and increase self-esteem.

During adolescence and young adulthood, several subjects need to be addressed. These constitute the basis of sexual education. Examples include:

- sex organs of both genders: names, functions, and concrete descriptions

- bodily changes that accompany puberty

- information on nocturnal emissions for boys and periods for girls

- intimacy: private and public settings

- sexual health: behaviors and initial examination of sexual organs/gynecological examination

- values and steps to decision-making

- communication about dating, love, intimacy and friendship

- how alcohol and drug use influence decision-making

- sexual intercourse and other sexual behaviors

- sexual orientation and identity

- birth control, menstruation, and the responsibilities of child-bearing

- condoms, contraception, and disease prevention

- emotions related to sexuality should be included in discussions since they motivate many behaviors.

The sociosexual educational program (Hénault, Forget and Giroux, 2003; Hénault, 2006) has been validated in more than twenty groups of adolescents and young adults with Asperger's and high-functioning autism. The proposed themes are divided into twelve workshops, which last ninety minutes each. The activities in each workshop are varied and elicit active participation from the participants. The themes not only reflect the experiences of participants, but also respect the criteria outlined by the National Information Center for Children and Youth with Disabilities (1992) and those defined by Haracopos and Pedersen (1999) and Kempton (1993). They include:

1. assessment and introduction to the program

2. introduction to sexuality and communication

3. love and friendship

4. physiological aspects and the sexual response cycle

5. sexual intercourse and other behaviors

6. emotions

7. STIs (sexually transmitted infections), HIV, and prevention

8. sexual orientation

9. alcohol, drugs, and sexuality

10. sexual abuse and inappropriate behaviors

11. sexism and violence

12. managing emotions, Theory of Mind, and intimacy.

Each workshop includes a support sheet for the group leader, the required materials, and all instructions. Activities can be adapted depending on the group (as a function of age, special needs, receptivity, etc.). In general, groups are created based on the participants' ages (from sixteen to twenty years, twenty to thirty years, thirty to forty years, etc.), and include both males and females. Boys are always curious to hear what girls think and vice versa. Although each workshop takes place over a ninety-minute period, a group leader could easily decide to divide it into two forty-five-minute workshops. Activities and exercises can also be repeated and extended over twenty workshops or more. Other modifications of the twelve-session pedagogical formula can also be made, according to the discretion of the group leader.

Materials can be adapted, both visually and practically, to help with the learning process. Films, computer programs, photos, diagrams, games, and Social Stories™ are referred to throughout the intervention. Sexual education can be offered in mixed groups (usually of between six and ten participants), but in cases where therapeutic interventions are combined with sexual education, individual sessions are preferable.

The educational program *Partners for Youth* (available at www. ucalcary.ca) is another useful resource for adolescents and adults with AS. In a simple and effective way, the individual is asked to reflect on different sorts of relations that can exist between two people. An initial questionnaire evaluates the basic knowledge of participants such as the appropriate time for affection, sexuality, and friendship. Depending on the results obtained, interpersonal relationships are explored in order to evaluate various limits of knowledge as well as abuse scenarios in the section called *About Relationships*. This tool includes many examples, suggestions, and resources. Throughout the interventions, individuals with AS are called to participate in a concrete way through role-play scenarios. Special capacities and strengths are encouraged, in order to maintain interest and motivation, including:

- notions of time and space: surroundings, behaviors, and individuals with whom intimate behavior is appropriate

- the limits of love (healthy, unhealthy, and abusive situations)

- what is dating violence? the cycle of violence

- how to react to sexual assault

- sexuality and the law: judge various situations and ask what is acceptable or unacceptable

- watch for warning signs: when someone is excessively jealous, has an explosive temper, becomes withdrawn or depressed, is extremely agitated, acts strangely, etc.

- how to prevent sexual abuse

- how to help a friend or yourself if you recognize aggressiveness.

CHAPTER 5

Conclusion

Individuals with ASD must receive guidance about sexual issues. An extended definition of sexuality takes into account factors linked to sexual development, puberty, and the symptoms associated with autism status. This positive approach respects the personal and cultural attitudes of individuals. Values are favored over an attitude of condemnation, which risks increasing social stigmas and taboos faced by individuals. Parents and professionals play a key role in terms of the education and media that they can offer.

An open and receptive attitude held by parents and professionals will pave the way for open communication and the opportunity for individuals with AS to share their experiences and issues, and express their concerns about sexuality.

To prevent the development of unsafe or illegal sexual behavior, we must first promote education and knowledge in people with AS. If left to themselves (with questions and curiosity about various sexual experiences, they may fall into the trap of looking at pornography on the internet. By giving them access to educational sites (Attwood, 2008), they will have answers to many questions, appropriate support for intervention, and recognition of their needs.

The sexual education and interventions programs not only aim to teach adolescents and adults to become responsible, but also offer them the necessary tools to develop interpersonal relationships. This process will therefore help them develop a healthy and enriching sexual lifestyle.

Sexual Guidelines for Organizations and Professional Services

Here is an example of sexual guidelines that are inspired by the work of the Center for Autism in Denmark (Haracopos, 2009) introduced in a Canadian Psychiatric Hospital (Taillefer *et al.*, 2013).

The guidelines are designed to orient and inform interventions targeting the emotional and sexual lives of people with AS. They take into account the particular personal context of the individual, with the aim of offering support and protection. Guidelines orient the thoughts and actions of everyday life. Emotional and sexual aspects of the person's life are considered, discussed, analyzed, and understood rather than avoided or ignored as a consequence of a lack of guidance or support from the family and professional caregivers.

More importantly, such guidelines also allow individuals to access sex education and thus reduce the risk of inappropriate or illegal conduct.

Objectives of the guidelines

- Acknowledge the right to an emotional and sexual life while taking into account the individual's psychological characteristics.

- Recognize the right to appropriate assessment and intervention related to disturbances in sexuality, especially if it threatens a successful integration in the social community.

- Obtain the services (assessment, information, training, support, treatment, therapy, etc.) required to improve the individual's emotional and sexual life.

- Clarify the attitudes and behaviors expected from professionals when facing diverse aspects of AS individual's emotional, romantic, and sexual behavior.

- Allow and support interventions in relation to the expression of emotional and sexual life, and problems and sexual dysfunction.

Realities and issues concerning the sexuality of people with AS

- AS individuals are often perceived as lifelong asexual children. This leads to overprotection and "over-sexualization" of the AS individual in response to the restrictions and limitations imposed by the environment. The risk is that the AS person may then act impulsively, without considering the environmental limits.

- The sexuality of people with autism and AS has been largely ignored.

- People with AS rarely have access to comprehensive sex education. The information received is usually focused on sexual behavior problems. There is little empirical data on the nature and frequency of adaptive sexual behavior.

- Families and peers of people with AS often have limited knowledge and experiences of sexuality.

- People with AS have limited access to appropriate and available educational resources.

- The families and caregivers are often uncomfortable when it comes to the sex lives of people with AS.

- Professionals sometimes tend to think they have the right to manage the sexual behavior of people with AS, without consulting the individual.

- Professionals tend to overprotect people with AS. Overprotection prevents any form of sexual expression.

- To protect vulnerable individuals, it is necessary to:

  - take into account their skills, level of maturity, and developmental age

  - give them the opportunity to make choices in terms of their social relations, their sexual expressions, contraception, and decisions regarding pregnancy.

In protecting individuals with AS, we advise professionals and families to act with prudence, promote sociosexual education, and provide support and assessment tailored to the needs of users. Taking the complexity of this subject into account, several factors must be considered:

- Protecting those who do not have the ability to make decisions linked to sexuality.

- Evaluating sexual consent as soon as required.

- Even if the person has the capacity to consent, that does not mean he/she will exercise appropriate and responsible sexual behavior.

- Sexual education or additional support could be beneficial for the person, but is not necessarily a prerequisite for sexual activity.

Vulnerability to sexual assault

Several vulnerabilities can contribute to the risk of sexual assault or to the expression of inappropriate sexual behavior, including:

- communication difficulties

- a lack of credibility

- a lack of knowledge and education about sexuality

- difficulty in detecting and recognizing a potential danger

- difficulty discriminating appropriate from inappropriate or criminal behaviors

- isolation

- need for affection and attention

- economical, physical, and psychological dependency

- deficits in interpersonal skills

- general tendency of submission and obedience to rules

- lack of decision-making power and control over their lives

- lack of self-esteem

- ignorance of the right to refuse to perform actions.

Proposed guidelines about some significant aspects of sexuality are listed below.

Masturbation

"Masturbation (sometimes called 'touching yourself', 'playing with yourself' or 'wanking', among many other terms) is when a person touches and fondles their own genitals (particularly the penis or clitoris) in a way that feels very nice to them, in response to sexual feelings and thoughts. After a few minutes, the feelings may become very exciting and intense, and result in an orgasm or pleasure" (Attwood, 2008). Various medical and psychological benefits have been attributed to a healthy attitude to sex in general and to masturbation in particular.

In this respect, educational intervention will help the person, the family, and the caregivers to know male and female means of masturbation and precisely identify places and safety and hygiene rules related to appropriate masturbation behavior.

If needed, a predetermined training program to learn correct masturbation behavior can be completed with the AS person, using the general guidelines described above. Intervention must be carefully designed to avoid taking up guilt-inducing intrusive educational attitudes.

Use of erotic material

In terms of intimate relationships, the objective is to promote personal interaction, to the extent of the ability and interest of the individual. When erotic material is used between partners, the notion of consent should also be respecteed and protected.

Pornography is a sympathetic portrayal of subjects and obscene information in an artistic, literary, or cinematic way. Scenes and photos show close-up images of genitals without representation of the people involved or the interaction between individuals. A pornographic film, also called an X-rated movie, is a film containing scenes of human intercourse shown explicitly and deliberately in order to excite the viewer, and using abusive language.

Erotic material respects greater sociosexual standards compared to pornography. Eroticism, or amorous desire, means all phenomena that arouse sexual desire, and various representations, particularly cultural and artistic, which express or arouse the senses. The eroticism may also designate, by extension, the nature of the relationship established between individuals due to this attraction. Scenes and photos show the body partially or totally nude without direct representation of genitals. The emphasis is on interaction and sexual desire, rather than on the images. The individuals represented in these images must be eighteen years of age or older.

Erotica includes objects or mediums used to stimulate or enhance arousal and sexual pleasure. This type of material can also be an alternative for someone who uses objects that could affect their health or personal safety (e.g. use of dangerous objects to masturbate). In this situation, the object should be replaced by safer equipment that achieves the same result. This support would be instructive and tailored to the individual, allowing him or her to make more appropriate choices that are less likely to cause harm. It is obviously important that the person be informed and educated with regard to the safety issues surrounding the use of such objects.

Given the profile and characteristics of individuals with AS, we must also pay attention to compulsive consumers of this kind of material in order to possibly help develop a less simplistic view of sexuality. The objective is to avoid contributing to the development of addictive behaviors when the individual with AS uses this type of equipment.

Bibliography

Ariel, C.N. (2012) *Loving Someone with Asperger's Syndrome: Understanding and Connecting with Your Partner.* Oakland, CA: New Harbinger Publications.

Aston, M.C. (2003) *Aspergers in Love.* London: Jessica Kingsley Publishers.

Aston, M. (2009) *The Asperger Couple's Workbook.* London: Jessica Kingsley Publishers.

Attwood, S. (2008) *Making Sense of Sex.* London: Jessica Kingsley Publishers.

Attwood, T. (1997) *Asperger's Syndrome: A Guide for Parents and Professionals.* London: Jessica Kingsley Publishers.

Basso, M.J. (1997) *The Underground Guide to Teenage Sexuality.* Minneapolis: Fairview Press.

Carnes, P. (1989) *Contrary to Love: Helping the Sexual Addict.* Minnesota: CompCare Publishers.

Carnes, P., Delmonico, D.L. and Griffin, E. (2007) *In the Shadows of the Net.* Minnesota: Hazelden.

Coleman, E. (1991) "Compulsive sexual behavior: new concepts and treatments." *Journal of Psychology and Human Sexuality 4*, 2, 37–52.

Durocher, L. and Fortier, M. (1999) *Programme d'Education Sexuelle [Sex Education Program].* Montréal: Les Centres Jeunesses de Montréal et la Régie Régionale de la Santé et des Services Sociaux, Direction de la santé publique. Centre Universitaire à Montréal.

Edmonds, G. and Worton, D. (2006) *The Asperger Love Guide.* London: Paul Chapman Publishing.

Ginevra, M., Nota, L. and Stokes, M. (unpublished) "The differential effects of autism and Down's syndrome upon sexual behavior." *Autism Research.*

Gray, S., Ruble, L. and Dalrymple, N. (1996) *Autism and Sexuality: A Guide for Instruction.* Indianapolis, IN: Autism Society of Indiana.

Griffiths, D., Quinsey, V.L. and Hingsburger, D. (1989) *Changing Inappropriate Sexual Behavior.* Baltimore, MD: Paul H. Brookes Publishing.

Griffiths, D., Richards, D., Fedoroff, P. and Watson, S.L. (2002) *Ethical Dilemmas: Sexuality and Developmental Disability.* New York: NADD Press.

Haracopos, D. (2009) *Policies, Ethics, Laws and Regulations.* Centre for Autism in Denmark Seminar: Sexuality and Autism. Athens, Greece.

Haracopos, D. and Pedersen, L. (1999) *The Danish Report.* Copenhagen: Society For The Autistically Handicapped.

Hellemans, H. (1996) *L'Education Sexuelle des Adolescents Autistes* [*Sex Education for Adolescents with Autism*]. Paper presented at Belgium Conference on Autism, Bruxelles.

Hellemans, H. and Deboutte, D. (2002) *Autism Spectrum Disorders and Sexuality.* Paper presented at World First Autism Congress, Melbourne.

Hénault, I. (2006) *Asperger's Syndrome and Sexuality.* London: Jessica Kingsley Publishers.

Hénault, I., Forget, J. and Giroux, N. (2003) *Le Développement d'Habiletés Sexuelles Adaptatives chez des Individus Atteints d'Autisme de Haut Niveau ou du Syndrome d'Asperger* [*Development of Adoptive Socio-sexual Skills for Individuals with High Functioning Autism or Asperger's Syndrome*]. Thèse présentée comme exigence partielle du Doctorat en Psychologie. University of Québec at Montréal.

Hendrickx, S. (2008) *Love, Sex and Long-Term Relationships: What People with Asperger Syndrome Really Really Want.* London: Jessica Kingsley Publishers.

Hingsburger, D. (1993) *Parents Ask Questions about Sexuality and Children with Developmental Disabilities.* Vancouver: Family Support Institute Press.

Hingsburger, D. (1995) *Hand Made Love: A Guide for Teaching About Male Masturbation Through Understanding and Video.* Newmarket: Diverse City Press.

Hingsburger, D. and Haar, S. (2000) *Finger Tips: Teaching Women with Disability About Masturbation Through Understanding and Video.* Newmarket: Diverse City Press.

Hollomotz, A. (2011) *Learning Difficulties and Sexual Vulnerability: A Social Approach.* London: Jessica Kingsley Publishers.

Holmes, D.L., Isler, V., Bott, C. and Markowitz, C. (2005) "Sexuality and individuals with autism and developmental disabilities." *Autism Spectrum Quarterly,* Winter–Fall, 30–33.

Kempton, W. (1993) *Socialization and Sexuality: A Comprehensive Training Guide.* California: W. Kempton.

Kempton, W. (1999) *Life Horizons I, II.* Santa Barbara, CA: James Stanfield Company.

Moreno, S., Wheeler, M. and Parkinson, K. (2012) *The Partner's Guide to Asperger's Syndrome.* London: Jessica Kingsley Publishers.

National Information Center for Children and Youth with Disabilities (1992) "Sexuality education for children and youth with disabilities." *NICHCY News Digest 17,* 1–37.

Partners for Youth (2011) Available at www.counselling.net/jnew/pdfs/handbooks-manuals-guides/PARTNERS%20FOR%20YOUTH,%20Making%20Waves%20=%20English.pdf, accessed May 13, 2014.

Ruble, L.A. and Dalrymple, J. (1993) "Social and sexual awareness of persons with autism: a parental perspective." *Archives of Sexual Behavior 22,* 229–240.

Taillefer, L., Langlois, L., Pommier, C., Prévost, M.J. and Hénault, I. (2013) *Lignes Directrices en Regard de la Vie Sexuelle [Sexual Guidelines for Patients at the Louis-H. Lafontaine Hospital: Psychiatry Program]*. Programme de psychiatrie en déficience intellectuelle de l'Hôpital L.H. Lafontaine.

Tremblay, G., Desjardins, J. and Gagnon, J.P. (1993) *Programme de Dévelopement Psychosexuel*. Eastman: Éditions Behaviora.

Index